Beating My Demons

Dave Casellas

DEDICATION

To anyone suffering from addiction or mental health conditions. Have you ever seen someone going "mad" in the street? Spare a thought for them and what led to that outburst.

CONTENTS

ACKNOWLEDGMENTS

To my wife and soul mate Lauretta and her mother Kathy. My greatest friend Mart who never expects anything in return. Mikey and all his family for putting up with me for all those years. All my friends from Teddington. And all the lads at QPR. For Noreen, Mary, Alan and Nicola. And a big blessing to my mum RIP. And of course my Dad and Viv back in Oz.

1 MEN IN WHITE COATS

Back in the day, there was an old expression… "The men in white coats will come to get you!" The men certainly came, not for me, but for my mum. This was the day that totally changed the whole path of my life. At the time I was uncertain whether it was a good or bad thing that happened. At the time I felt confused, devastated, scared and also a little relieved. I was 14 or 15 years old, and at that moment life was horrific. I could never have expressed that to anyone, I did not know how to. I had become a rebel, but a petrified one at that. So what had led to mum being taken away? it had been a long time in coming and very sadly so. In a nutshell, mum was by her own admission an alcoholic, a violent one at that. She was already under the care of psychiatric services. I remember a male nurse, he was Irish and his name was Tony.

For some reason I hated him, only out of an undeserved loyalty for mum. He would arrive every two weeks or monthly if my memory serves me. They would go into the front room, mum would scream and swear at Tony, and I could make out he was giving mum an injection.

I can only guess that the injection was to calm mum down, well it certainly wasn't working!

Back to the point I was getting at, the men in white coats. The last time Tony arrived, he was with two other men, and they were in White coats, believe it or not. They dragged mum away, screaming to a van outside. My little sister was hysterical; it was a very traumatic experience. Somehow I kept very cool under the circumstances, maybe I was in shock. There was also a woman present who led my sis away. I asked Tony where she was going, he replied he did not know.

Now if you were to define a moment that was the moment my little messed-up family was destroyed. It was at least a year before I saw my sis again, maybe longer. I will go into that a bit more later on.

I can't really remember who took me, possibly Tony, anyway I was taken to a home for delinquent lads called Grafton Lodge. .

I was born in Perth, Western Australia, June 1967. My father is Australian of Spanish origin, his mother was Australian, of English and Austrian origin.

My mum was English; her real father was Scottish and her mother English. So there I have a mixed heritage, barbarian like!

Mum had met my Dad in London; I was actually conceived in Cricklewood, NW London. They went to Australia where I was born. Mum was never happy in Oz, I found out many years later she sort of kidnapped me and bought me back to London, much to Dads dismay. He followed back but never really wanted to.

Dad had been a professional Australian Rules footballer, but had to retire very early through injury. He became a sports journalist and had even appeared on TV on a weekly Aussie football show.

Mum had worked for Cunard shipping on the big ocean liners, she was very intelligent also.

My early memories are few and far between, we lived in Teddington, near Twickenham. My sis was born when I was four years old. Even as little baby I remember her fiery red hair. As she grew older she looked like little orphan Annie, I used to take the mick by calling her Ronald McDonald. This would have been early 1970s; McDonalds would have been fairly new to the UK.

We ended up moving to a massive house again in Teddington right next to the NPL... the laboratories where the famous bouncing bomb for the Dambusters had been invented.

Bushy Park was right there as well, a magical place where there were deer, stags, a boating pond and trees and ferns everywhere. Bushy Park was full of big craters in the ground where bombs in WW2 had landed. Eisenhower has his HQ in Teddington. A bit of history there for you!

I was no older than eight years old when Dad decided to leave, he told me many years later the reason he did so. This was a memory that I had subconsciously left out that I also found out later.

I obviously must have been devastated; I didn't see Dad again for over a year. I remember being at school in the playground when it was home time and seeing a tall, dark handsome man in a crombie overcoat striding along. It was Dad, he had finally come to pick me up and see me. I was overjoyed.

Dad had met another woman, Lynn, she made it

clear she never wanted children, and didn't really like myself or my sister being around. The times we went to see Dad, we always ended up in a pub or a beer garden depending on the weather. Dad lived in a small studio flat up at Parliament Hill. His local was the pub which Ruth Ellis had used, the last lady hung in Britain for murder.

I used to like going up to that neck of the woods, there was a massive adventure playground on the heath and an open air lido.

Dad would go out up the road for a pint or two on a Saturday night, and I would be left in to watch Match of the Day. I would have cereal, always with long life milk; I grew to love the taste of that carton milk. As a youngster my team was Manchester United, they were one of the best, just at the end of George Best's era. Then for some reason, I fell in love with QPR, Stan Bowles was still playing at that time. Who wouldn't be in awe of a colourful player and character like him! This brings me on to when Mum had a new man in her life, Patrick. He was an Irishman who loved rugby. He was a former player of London Irish who were then based in Sunbury. They were both always in the pub and always drunk, although mum seemed the worse for wear out of the two of them.

Many a night, my sister and me were left in the back of Patrick's car while they drank the night away in the pub. We were supplied with crisps and a small glass bottle of coca cola and a straw. That was us for hours, the night seemed endless. Then after a while we no longer went in the car, we were just left indoors. My sister and I would spend hours sat up by the window, just looking out in the hope of mum coming home. And to be honest when they did come back I wish they hadn't. More often than not mum would start screaming at Patrick, and I often witnessed mum hitting him and even saw her stub her cigarette on his face. It was horrific and very scary; mum was like a raging mad woman. I could always smell red wine on her breath and in the air. Fair play to Patrick he never hit mum back, but I still hated him, or maybe I had an ounce of a soft spot for him. This went on for what was possibly a few years, we lived in a ground floor maisonette, and people lived above us, they must have heard all the violence.

Sometimes I would cry and scream when the fighting started; a few times I took a severe beating from mum.

I started my school life at Teddington Comprehensive School for boys, a secondary school; beginning at aged eleven years old. The first two years I mixed with lads with what seemed very good home lives. Their families seemed normal; they were to some degree what I would deem as well spoken and fairly well off. They were good friends; I was in the top classes so I was fairly intelligent. My best subject was English Language; I was good at writing and using words.

My home life as I have already explained was horrible. I rebelled somewhat against my mother, and also at this period of time, Punk rock was all the rage.

I met my best mate, who still is to do this very day. Martin, we met in the second year of school. He always wore a mohair jumper and had spikey-ish hair. If I was to compare Mart to a punk icon of the time it would be Jonny Rotten, John Lydon of the Sex Pistols.

Every Friday, I was invited to Mart's house in Whitton, near to the Twickenham rugby stadium, or not far anyway. Mart's mum would make burger and chips, followed by ice cream. This was a treat, I looked forward to that, and it was like normality to me. I would only be home alone with my sis while mum was getting drunk. That was how it seemed at the time.

We were twelve years old; it was all about music and football. Mart also used to wear a Spurs second shirt, the yellow one. Somehow I convinced Mart to support my team, QPR. We became two peas in a pod, hardly ever apart. I had now left my upper class buddies behind and loved the excitement of being a punk rebel. Mart got me into groups like the Stranglers, the Damned, UK Subs and many more.

Another great friend I had around that time was Gifford; he had a lovely mother who was a single mum. Gifford's dad was West Indian and had left. Gifford loved the Clash, so this was another band I started to enjoy. I spent a lot of time at Gifford's; back in those days lads would be out and about a lot more. Not like the tech era we have now, most kids spend all their time on a mobile phone, computer or gaming. We were in the open, getting muddy and up to all sorts of mischief.

Myself, Martin, Gifford and a few others started to get involved with glue sniffing. Another term is solvent abuse, we did not see any dangers or in fact had never been warned or educated about any potential harm this would cause.

There were a couple of places we would go to get out of our heads on the glue. Teddington back in the 80's was a lot different from how it is now. I suppose that is the case with nearly every area. Teddington had two main streets that were separated by a railway bridge; Broad Street and High Street. The rail station was right there by the bridge, under the bridge was a little shed like building, it was now disused, just along was the coal yard, which has now been long gone. There was an old two seat settee and a chair in this dilapidated outhouse. It was musky and damp, it probably stank, but we didn't care about things like that.

All of us lads would have looked older than we were and were able to buy glue in the local hardware stores. It was either that or shop keepers back in those days were a lot more relaxed about licensing laws. We also got served cider which I will go into llater on.

There were two brands of glue that we used, EvoStick and Thixofix. The glue would be poured into a plastic bag and inhaled deeply and rapidly. The affects from the glue were amazing, it would take affect immediately, and the hallucinations were vivid and seemed real. It would be a mix of funny things and scary visions. It was a complete escape from reality and we would spend hours tripping in another world. There were a couple of hairy moments, one which stands out is when Mart was hallucinating and thought he was stuck in the wall and only his arms and legs were sticking out from the brickwork. We snapped him out of it. Another lad we all knocked about with was Mikey; he was tall just like Gifford 6 foot 3 I would say. Gifford and Mikey often had little fall outs with each other, a bit of a rivalry thing I would say. Probably the maddest vision I had on glue; I was sitting with Mart on the filthy old settee, silently and in our own fantasy worlds. Gifford was in the chair, in walked Mikey and a row started about what, I'll never know. They both squared up and Mikey landed a punch straight to Gifford's jaw. Now the way I saw that event was like something from a horror movie. It was my own personal film right there in front of my eyes! The hallucination I witnessed was that Mikey had turned into Frankenstein and Gifford was Dracula. Frankenstein had hit Dracula so hard that his head had been knocked clean of his shoulders. That freaked me right out to be honest and took a good few minutes to get back into reality from that one.

Firstly I was a punk as I said before, there was a barber shop in Teddington High Street that we all used, Ken's, he was great character always friendly and welcoming of us young Herbert's. I suppose we gave him a lot of business.

I had a great Mohican style haircut by Ken; I used to spike it up by using soap. The first day I turned up at school I was suspended and had to get it cut off. And the day I got my new style I walked back home, my sis was in the kitchen by the window. I crept up to the window and peered in at her, she jumped out of her skin bless her. I must have looked a bit scary, maybe that was the image I was trying to achieve, part of my rebellion.

While a few of us were punks most of the older lads had turned into skinheads. The older mob had a name for their gang, the Cockney Cowboys. I can't remember if they had taken the name from SHAM 69's hit single "Hersham Boys" or it was just a coincidence. Anyway most of the lads supported Chelsea and Brentford, much to my dismay. There were a few of us that were QPR, and gradually I had started to recruit some of the lads to support the R's.

The cockney cowboys used to knock around in a big old derelict house, which was nicknamed The Squat. The squat was right next to St Albans church, which was more like a small cathedral, very high roof all made of lead and also at the time was disused and very eerie inside. If there was such things as ghosts, then this place was where they would be. The famous Norwegian band AHA made a video for one of their hits in St Albans church.

The squat was like an HQ for the gang and all us younguns. We would be served bottles of cider from the pub up the road which had a serving hatch and was allowed to sell take away booze. The elders drank and we sniffed our glue.

Another great friend around this time was Derek, also a punk, he was tall and has almost modelled himself on Sid Vicious, always wearing black leathers and had black spiky hair. A lot of girls knocked around with us too. On some weekend we would have a group of up to thirty of us causing havoc around the squat. Sometimes the Cockney Cowboys would head into Kingston to fight gangs there and come back to tell the tails of their battles. We looked up to them and they would often kick us into shape, in a way this was to toughen us up a kind of rough nurturing. My favourite piece of clothing at the time was a dark brown sheepskin coat, which I am sure Patrick had either given to me or he had left it when he had eventually parted from my mum. I must have looked a right scruff, as the coat was covered in glue stains from our sniffing escapades.

2 FINDING MY FISTS

It was during my time at school that I started to be bullied by one particular lad. This boy seemed to think he was a bit hard; he was a skinhead at the time. What with all the hell that was going on at home with mum and Patrick, it had affected me subconsciously. My appearance was not great, I had started to become a punk rocker, and I wore an old jumper which was not part of the uniform. I was quiet and also was not quite like all the other boys at that time. Most kids of that age had started to smoke or at least experimented and tried a cigarette. A group would smoke behind the bike sheds or even brazenly take a puff in the toilets, until a teacher would furiously come in and herd us all out amid all the smoke lingering in the air.

I would sneakily take cigarettes from mum's packets, she was too drunk to realize, and I would sometimes take a few quid from her purse so I could buy chips at lunch time or after school.

The lad I mentioned would keep calling me names, about how scruffy I was and he knew I had smokes in my pocket. He would threaten me and take cigarettes. This happened a few times. The final straw for me was when he demanded money from me. I had had enough, I stood up to him. I offered to fight him one break time; we arranged a time and a place. We were to go to the side of the sports hall out the back of the playground the next lunchtime.

I told the others in my class, and word got round. I could hardly sleep that night, I was nervous as hell. I kept visualizing how the fight would go; I was telling myself I was going to take a beating: but I had to go through with it.

The morning came, and to say my stomach was churning would be an understatement. I could not concentrate on any of the class work that morning, all I had on my mind was to beat the dickhead who had been terrorizing me.

Finally the bell went for lunch, my comrades in my class stayed close behind me. The other boy was a lot more popular than me and had all the older lot and the harder lads in our year behind him like an entourage you see at a big boxing event.

We went over to the agreed area, which was out of sight of the teachers on duty in the playground. This was it, I had so much pent up aggression inside of me, and this was to be a release of all the hurt and fear I was experiencing in my life away from school. There was a massive crowd surrounding us, I was aware that some lads had spat at my back as we entered the arena.

We squared up to each other... Bang! I just gave my aggressor the best punch I could muster and it landed straight on his eye socket. I saw his cheekbone swell straight up; I steamed into him raining blows to his head and face. I had a superhuman strength inside me that came from nowhere.

The roar and shouting of a hundred or so schoolboys had alerted the teachers; they ran over and broke us up. They were maybe even angrier than I felt, I was manhandled and marched off, and the fight was over in less than a minute I would say.

The baying mob that had been supporting the bully boy looked in total shock. And my classmates looked in total shock and in a kind of awe of what had just happened. David v Goliath, I was the victor. I felt like a king right now, a massive release and a feeling of absolute excitement and relief.

Back in those days caning was still allowed in schools, so I received my punishment and a stern telling off. My communication skills were non existent; I could not express why I had this fight to the teachers or even mum. I do not know if mum had any idea or even any self realization as to why my behaviour was changing for the worse.

That afternoon I went back to class, I received a hero's welcome, and some of the boys commented they could not believe I was able to defeat the clear favourite. After that I had earned a respect from the others, and I had been accepted by my opposition.

All I can say about that event, it changed me completely. In my eyes that was the way to be accepted, or be anyone.

Throughout all these times, I never spoke about what was going on in indoors and mums drunkenness and anger. The only person that really knew a bit about it was Mart.

I started to become a lot more of a delinquent and

started to be involved with the law. One incident we were picked up by the police and bundled in the back of a van because we were seen glue sniffing. While we were locked in the back of the van our mothers were called. They could only get hold of Marts mum; my mum was probably drunk in the pub as usual. We drove toward Twickenham and we still had a pot of glue in one of our pockets. We couldn't get rid because the doors were firmly locked. It was dark and very cold, the van came to a halt and a couple of the coppers opened up the double doors. There was Marts mum peering in, in disgust. She saw the tin of glue rolling around in the back and went ballistic. We were taken to Twickenham police station. Mart was probably warned and taken home by his mum. I had to wait in a back room while they traced my old dear. I was panicking and scared that mum was going to turn up and make a massive drunken scene. I saw a door was open in the courtyard where the van had parked. I made a dash for it and legged it as fast as I could back toward Teddington. I was apprehended within ten minutes, the irony was this was my first escape form the police.

Mum eventually surfaced, and as I knew she would be steaming drunk. Surprisingly I didn't get much of a ticking off, but the whole incident was a total embarrassment, but to be honest I really didn't care that much.

Mart's mum banned me from going round their house after that, so no more burger and chips, I was well gutted. There was a time one Friday that Mart's mum was out and we managed to get a ladder, so I sneaked in through a window at the back garden. A neighbour must have seen this and alerted the police thinking I was a burglar. This double cemented my ban from the house!

It was when I was around 14 years old that I got my first girlfriend, Jane. Mart kind of went out with her friend Claire. Myself and the two girls were skinheads; Mart always at that time remained a punk. This was just before we turned casual.
The years that Patrick had spent with mum, he had started to take me to see QPR over at Shepherds Bush. I am not sure whether he actually wanted to, or it was some kind of duty to keep mum happy. The first time I saw Loftus Road was when Patrick had driven up there and my memory tells me it was a Sunday afternoon when there was no game being played.

Around QPR's ground is a series of streets with rows of terraced houses. Right in the middle of these streets, oh and a school at one end, hence the name for the away end of the ground; "The School End". The year would have been 1977, the ground looked to be made of blue corrugated iron, its appearance was awesome to me, and the tall floodlights in each corner. I was so excited; I wanted to be in there right at that moment. However it was silent and had a kind of eeriness to the place. I wonder if that had been a surveillance mission for Patrick to see where the ground was and case out the parking situation.

The first ever game Patrick took me to at Loftus Road was v Wolves, we lost 1-3. A certain player, Bob Hazell a massive Jamaican defender stood out as one of the best players that evening. He later went on to play for QPR.

It didn't seem to bother me too much that we lost; it was just a privilege for me to be there among the crowd. Patrick took us in the School End for away fans a big terrace behind the goal. I was aware there were other QPR fans dotted around in that end.

The next game I was taken to was away at Chelsea at Stamford Bridge. Patrick did not drive there; this must have been one of my first experiences on an Underground train. The train ran up right by the side of the ground it looked huge, a lot bigger than

Loftus Road. My heart was pounding through my chest in excitement and awe as we entered into the ground. The terrace was big, steep and curved; a lot of the steps seemed to be crumbling with grass and weeds growing everywhere. We stood right up the back with all the other QPR fans situated next to a covered stand for the home fans. QPR were playing all in red, the away kit. We won 3-1 this time; the pitch looked in a terrible state, which added to the experience, this was football at its best in the 70s.

We went to a few more games at Loftus Road, always night games in midweek, this was because Patrick would always be at London Irish on a Saturday and mum would be with him.

QPR were relegated to the Second Division, and I was in awe of all the singers in the Loft end of the ground. They were very loyal, cheering on the team even though we kept losing.

The year would now be 1980; myself and Mart had started to go to games together. There was about five of us would get a bus, one of the old Routemaster London double deckers, which used to go all the way from Teddington to Camden Town in those days. We would all get off at Hammersmith and make our way over to the home of our beloved team in Shepherds Bush.

The casual scene had started to take shape, a lot of lads and even girls too began to wear colourful and smart clothing. It was mainly golfing jumpers and tennis sports wear. Brands such as Pringle, Lyle and Scott, Slazenger, Fila, Ellesse, Taccini and other brands. It was a very smart look, and I was a bit jealous that I could not afford such attire.

God bless my mum, all her money would go on the booze, I would get a bit of pocket money, but I suppose it wasn't enough for my needs. When I was still at junior school, I got involved in a bit of shoplifting, myself and another mate created a "Nicking Club". We would steal sweets from a corner shop near to our school. It was more of a daring hobby than anything else. Every item we took, we would log and enter into a little book, like the cash register books which were lined. I stupidly had left that book in the playing area by the school. It had my name in the book, and it was handed to police by whoever found it.

That was my first experience of being dealt with by the law. Obviously mum was dismayed, but could not see the reasons for my behaviour at the time. I was never destined to be a career criminal, I mean who would keep a log of stolen items with their name in it!

Anyway back to the football; Leeds away early 80s, myself and Mart went up on the train, we won 1-0. Everyone was in great spirits on the way back. We had a bottle of cider to drink, and it was around the time of the end of our glue sniffing career. I was wearing my old faithful soiled sheepskin coat, and had a skinhead shaved head. The older lads on the train had already turned casual, wearing smarter clobber as I mentioned before. Another defining memory and turning point was one of the fellas, a big black lad, Lionel congratulated Mart and I for being good lads. But Lionel told us straight, well the comment was more aimed at me. "You need to smarten up; you look like a paraffin lamp" (slang for tramp!). I could have taken that really badly and never came back, but it was a kick up the backside I needed, and because of the respect we had for those chaps, we decided we would shape up and try and get cleaner and smarter.

I kept pestering mum for some money so I could get some clothing, bless her finally she gave in and I had enough to buy a Patrick rain jacket or cagoule as they were called. I felt the part in this coat; I was now part of the casual scene.

There was nothing like the buzz and bravado of hundreds of blokes all walking in a mob together dressed and feeling invincible.

My first experience of football violence at QPR was in 1980, a bit before I turned casual. Me and Mart would go to as many games as we could, we would somehow find the money for entrance fee, bus fare and a bottle or two of Cider.

Goldhawk Road in Shepherds Bush had a record exchange, all the vinyl records of the time and tapes etc. We had built up a collection of Punk and Skinhead albums. On the Saturdays of the home games we would head straight to the shop. We would trade in our prized albums and get cash back. Just over the road by Goldhawk Road underground station was a grotty little café. Our ritual was to have a sausage sarnie smothered in brown sauce and a cup of Rosie Lee, topped with grease floating on top! After our pre match snack we would somehow get served in an off license and buy a couple of litre bottles of Old English cider. This was enough to get us merry.

The game in question was Cardiff City at home. We were playing well and we won 2-0. We always went in the Loft, the home end behind the goal; mostly we would stand right over in the corner because it was less packed. On this day we decided to go up the back right behind the goal. The game had only just started and all of a sudden three mad geezers shouted out they were Cardiff. A few people backed off and then some older lads got involved and it all kicked off. After the match we noticed that all the lads started heading toward where the Cardiff fans were making their way back to coaches and to White City station, a long walk back up South Africa Road. There was a lot of tension and we saw a lad get smashed over the head with a brick, he ended up out cold in the gutter. QPR and Cardiff fans were fighting all the way down the road. We did not get involved that day, but just to watch the ferocity of the aggro was exciting to us.

As I said before, Mart lived in Whitton and I was in Teddington. There was a council estate off the Kingston Road in Teddington and we had loads of mates from school that lived there. We would play football in a caged enclosure and also get pissed on cider. We made homemade tattoos with Indian ink and a sewing needle.

One of the younger lads Lee had very kind loving parents and they would take in Foster kids. Lee's father was Mick, an absolute salt of the earth. He was a stone mason and had a Sherpa van. Mick would take half a dozen of us to the away games. We had a great camaraderie and laugh; we went to places like Barnsley, Rotherham, Cambridge and Wolverhampton.

As we got older me and Mart would start going away on our own, hence the time at Leeds away when we decided to become casual.

We convinced the girls to come to QPR away at Crystal Palace. This would have been 1981 again. We got the over ground train over from Clapham Junction. We had our obligatory cider, and to be with three good friends was great. I wanted to impress Jane that day, but that was not to be, or that was what I thought anyway.

We stood in the big open terrace at Selhurst Park in the corner which housed the away fans. The atmosphere was tense and we joined in the singing, the game wasn't dull, I can't remember the score it was either 0-0 or we lost, still a good game though. Something weird happened right at the end of the match. In the corner of the seats which was to the right of us, about a hundred blokes all older and looking quite mean to be honest walked down the steps into the seats chanting Millwall, "No one likes us". What were Millwall fans doing at a Palace v QPR game?

All the older QPR lot who had gathered up the back

of the terrace waiting to get out early and go looking for the Palace now looked a bit sheepish. We held back a bit to see what happened. Millwall had a fierce reputation for trouble, and the Palace fans in those seats did nothing to oppose them even though they had walked into their end. What was our lot going to do about this unexpected situation?

The final whistle was blown and everyone started to pour out of the ground like ants on a mission. We turned right out of the ground; we could not see our older lads. As we walked along in the throng of the crowd, we heard an almighty roar go up. Our fans who were mainly normal supporters started running in our direction. To be honest this was a scary situation, this was not in the day's plans for sure. The girls and us had to follow suit and get out of there, I certainly didn't want a beating from some grizzly looking Millwall fans, and this was supposed to be a day when I won Jane over! We darted into a front garden and hid behind a wall, so much for our bravado ha-ha.

The main hoards of fans had dispersed apart from the one's that had held back to let the stampede through. We surfaced from behind the wall and to our relief the danger was over. We headed on to

Selhurst station. When we made our way down the platform, much to our delight, it was full of QPR fans, still no sign of our main mob, I still to this day never found out what happened to that lot. All the talk was about what had happened and how surprised and relieved we were to still be in one piece. The train pulled in and we all boarded, we were headed back to Clapham. There was a solemn atmosphere on the carriage and one of apprehension as well. Was the danger over?

Next stop was Thornton Heath, the train pulled in and the doors opened. Around twenty men in their thirties, who all looked like mountains to us little teenagers burst on to the carriage. Our carriage was full of families and fathers with their sons. The lot that had rudely charged on the train had chanted that they were Palace, and snatched QPR scarves from some of the kids as though they had taken scalps as some kind of trophy. I just wished that we could have done something, but we were too young and we were still reeling from having to hide from the Millwall herd.

I did not go out with Jane for long, I was more interested in football and fighting and generally being a teenage terror. The 1980's was an era when most lads were getting involved in trouble at football; there was also the miners strike and the Falklands War all going on around this era.

The season 1982-83 was probably my favourite ever as a QPR fan. Myself and Mart went to nearly every game home and away. QPR were playing on the infamous Astroturf which admittedly gave us an advantage. We had got to the FA Cup final the season before, which was a fantastic experience. The FA Cup back in those days had a certain magic about it, the old Wembley stadium with vast packed terraces and the old twin towers.

Back to 82-3, we played some great football and eventually we were champions of the old second division. Violence at football was in it's heyday, every week would be some kind of trouble. It was like an element of danger which gave me the excitement. The last three home games of the season were against Leeds, Fulham and Wolves. At each of these games we invaded the pitch and there was loads of fighting inside and out of the ground.

I could probably write another book on the stories and memories of football, there are so many books out there written by the various teams firms.

To this very day I still try and get to some games,

but to be honest that feeling inside me of total excitement has sadly gone. Maybe the big games such as the Wembley Play Off Final against Derby and the odd London derby day can produce that emotion in me.

3 ON THE FARM

As I've mentioned before, mum had been taken and sectioned under the mental health act. Mum had spent time in locked wards and in and out all the time, at the time I had no concept or idea what she was going through. I only saw her as an embarrassment, when she kicked off in public I just wanted to be swallowed up by the ground. I had to witness some horrible things when she was drunk, I hated her, but more out of total fear than anything else.

After sis was taken into foster care and I spent the time in the lads' home, mum was re-housed and given a tenancy in a two bed flat on Butts Farm estate. Butts Farm was a big sprawling council estate in between Feltham and Whitton, Middlesex. The area had a tough old reputation back then, a lot of travellers lived round the area. The big block of flats which was long rather than a high rise building was right next to a big field alongside the A316 Chertsey Road.

There were burned out cars which had been stolen and old tyres everywhere. The older lads would race round on scrambling bikes, and had developed a track and jumps, like a motocross circuit.

I had left school and got my first ever job. It was a job that was sort of forced on me by the Job Centre. I was a packer/ dispatcher for computer circuit boards in a Factory in Feltham. I could walk to work so that was a positive; at least I didn't have to wait for a bus first thing in the morning.

Mum was getting involved with some serious drinking buddies; they were like characters from the TV series "Shameless". I dreaded being at home, mum attracted dossers who would often sleep in the other bedroom while mum stayed downstairs with her boyfriend, a scrounger called Jim. I hated Jim with a vengeance, all I saw was him getting mum pissed all the time, they lived in squalor, his flat was like an open recycle container for empty cans. The place stank of piss, and mum was permanently out of her head. She would have been drinking on top of all the medication that was supposed to be keeping her calm. Jim didn't care about my mum, he just used her. I found out that he would take my mum's giro cheque from Social Security, and cash it up and just buy booze with it.

I asked Mart, would he come as a back up for me, I was going to beat the shit out of Jim. We marched down there one evening and knocked on the door; Jim came to the door, I said no words and just steamed into him. I punched him till he fell to the ground and Mart booted him so hard, to this day he swears he broke his foot with the force of the kick.

I had now turned 17 years old, it was 1983. Back in those days a week's wages was enough for me to go to the pub nearly every night and still have money to go to football and maybe save for the odd bit of clothing. I had saved enough to buy a striped Lacoste polo shirt that I really liked. I was made-up with my new item, it had brown, yellow and green stripes and was quite rare, I had not seen many of the boys at QPR wear one of these. I only wore it a couple of times, to discover it had gone missing from the flat. I asked mum had she seen it, she told me she had hung it out to dry on the landing on our block. I could not believe it that would have lasted a matter of minutes before being thieved.

Mum had also had a little Yorkshire terrier taken from around that block of flats. If you fell asleep around that area someone would have taken your eyes out and come back for your eyelashes later.

I spent most nights in Twickenham in the pubs. I would always get up for work in the morning. I first started going in pubs when I was 16 years old, either the landlords didn't care or I looked older than my age.

Fighting was the norm for me, I had no idea how to chat girls up, or even chat at all, and I was a kid with very few words. I did all my talking with my fists. Mart was similar to me, not so violent but also very quiet. We didn't really need to talk; we just did things to amuse ourselves, which usually ended in bother.

There was a pub in Twickenham, The Red Lion, and a lot of the Whitton lads drank there. The cockney cowboys would also come over and then there was the Twickenham lot. Some were still skinheads and had never turned casual. We would play pool and listen to the duke box. Most of the fellas in there were Chelsea which annoyed me; I just had to deal with it.

One night there was a big row outside the pub, I can't remember who or what it was about, I just recollect that police were called, and I hit one of them. I escaped being arrested that night.

The morning after, I went to work as usual, and before lunch time two uniformed police arrived and strode into the office. I saw the boss pointing over in my direction and they sternly walked toward me. My heart was pounding like a jack-hammer.

"David Casellas?" the copper knew it was me, but I'm sure they just loved to re-iterate the point. Anyway I was nicked and taken outside into a parked police car. My colleagues looked on in astonishment; I bet they had not expected something like this to happen on a drab Thursday morning.

I was charged with assaulting the police, I am still not sure how they got my name, either I was grassed up or the pub landlord had found out my name. I was taken to Feltham Magistrates Court and remanded in custody, now this was a situation I never thought I would find myself in.

I had no idea what to expect, one thing I did know was that it wasn't going to be a bed of roses. Firstly I was put in cuffs and taken out to the courtyard where a sweatbox was awaiting our departure. A sweat box was the term for a prison van; it was long with single compartments, just enough room to seat one person. It had a caged window like wire mesh, with a very stiff uncomfortable seat. This vehicle had to go round various courts in West London to pick up other unlucky travellers. The window was literally a slit with tinted glass, so no one outside could see our happy faces leering out at them. I sat there in solitary confinement playing a game with myself, trying to guess what roads we were going down. It was a bit like learning the knowledge to become a London cabbie, only without the freedom.

I'm sure our last stop was South Western magistrates, Lavender Hill. The passengers in this elongated one star coach were far from happy customers. There was a lot of shouting and lads asking for a "burn". I later learned that a burn was a roll up cigarette, for obvious reasons.

We had driven up toward the West End of London and I worked out we were near Waterloo station somewhere. The van turned into what looked like a multi story car park, only there was a lot more room to maneuver this vehicle inside. It was very dim and dark, and I could see there were half a dozen other vans just like this already parked up in a row. One of the vans was off loading a load of fellas, some young and some a lot older, they were all being led in handcuffs through a big double door into god knows where.

Our van was next to be emptied out, my door was opened and a chirpy old fella who looked like a security guard put the cuffs on me which were chained to his own wrist. He led me through the doors into the magic grotto. Only I wasn't going to see Santa, I was probably being introduced to Satan! Would this be like entering the gates of hell! Just ahead of us was another man who looked remarkably like the guy leading me, he was sitting at a desk. There was a big white-board on the wall with a load of names with numbers next to them.

"Casellas", my escort announced to the serious looking official. He looked straight at me and replied... "Latchmere House" in a matter of fact tone of voice.

I did not know where or what Latchmere House was all I did know was I was very glad I wasn't going to Feltham. Everyone had heard of Feltham. That had a very bad reputation for violence and bullying. Feltham was right near where I lived, but I could not have wanted to be any further away from that gaff.

It appeared that there were cell doors, each with a prison name printed on a notice above each one.

Brixton, Wormwood Scrubs, Pentonville, Wandsworth; these were the big boys prisons. I was thankfully only 17, so in the eyes of the justice system I was a juvenile, not yet an adult.

Then came the cells for Feltham, Chelmsford and my door Latchmere House. The door clanked open and as I entered what was in theory a huge police cell with benches all around the walls of the room. Three sides of the walls were taken up with around twenty other lads all around my age. Most of the boys were black, and a lot of them were built a lot bigger then me! I tried not to make any eye contact, but what I did pick up on was a very tense and volatile atmosphere. I kind of worked out that all these inmates were not at all chuffed at being here.

I sat myself down on the emptiest bench and kept my head down. This was my first experience of going to jail and I had an expression before of "keeping your nut down" and staying quiet. I did indeed say nothing, and no one said anything to me, thankfully. There was a group of around half a dozen black lads who all seemed to know each other very well. If I am to be honest I was scared and I did my best not to show it. A lot of the lads had plastic bags full of belongings with them. I had nothing with me, just myself. Back in those days there were no mobile phones or IPods or such like.

There was a lot of chat about how these boys had got on in court and the various offences they were up for. Robbery was a popular theme as was GBH and other serious crimes. Here I was for just being a dick outside a pub in leafy Twickenham. Most of these lads were from inner London, places like Battersea, Brixton and Camden Town.

A lad who did look like he was showing his fear was sitting and fidgeting on the bench, he had a radio with him. And it was not long before he was set upon and had his radio "taxed" from him. Taxed was a term in the early 80s for robbing or taking items from a person. And in that era a lot of taxing went on in the streets for expensive clothing that had either just been purchased from a shop or straight off a victims back. In this case it was this poor souls' only possession, his radio. I felt for this bloke, he made no effort to protect his property or himself, he just gave it up and stared at the floor, he clearly did not want any trouble.

We all sat there for what seemed like an eternity; eventually the big iron door opened up and we were all called out one by one. We were herded back into another sweatbox and crammed into our own cubicles. The van pulled out of the concrete building out onto the busy street that leads up to Westminster Bridge. The sky was black it was a winter's night and all the rush hour traffic was now starting to die down a bit. People all going about their daily routines were hurrying along the busy pavements back to their homes. I felt very alone right now and also fearful about what to expect on my arrival at Latchmere House. I wondered if my mum had even been informed, or whether she had even been able to be contacted. She was more than likely lying drunk with that leech of a man Jim.

It took about an hour or so to reach our destination; Latchmere House was not a Victorian style prison like the Scrubs, Wandsworth or Brixton. It had two main blocks and a reception building. Tall wire fences topped with razor wire surrounded the prison. It seemed a strange place to have a place like this; it was right in the middle of a leafy suburb known as Ham and Petersham. Tommy Steele lived round here somewhere, and the rest of the residents would not have been short of a few bob.

Latchmere during this period was a remand centre for juveniles and one block for convicted prisoners. The blocks were two stories high and were corridors with cells for two men next to each other. The reception process was quite humiliating, I had to strip naked and give all my clothing and any belongings to the officer behind the desk. There were a few other officers around and a couple of inmates who were in prison uniforms. They were probably lads that had landed a cushy job and were out of their cells.

The number that I had seen written next to my name back at Lambeth was my new prison number. I was issued with prison kit, brown denim trousers and traditional blue pinstripe shirt, just like Ronnie Barker wore in Porridge. I later found out that unconvicted inmates wore brown denim and convicted lads wore blue. Some of the lads wore their own clothes on remand, which their families or friends would bring in on visits.

My first ever night spent in Her Majesty's hotel was not as bad as I thought it would be. I was banged up with a lad who seemed ok, so that was a result. We were taken over to a big dining area with long tables and had an evening tea. Everything was made of plastic, the cutlery; cups and plates were all blue plastic. Everything in prison was blue, except for the brown denims.

I had been remanded for three weeks and had to go back to Feltham Magistrates Court for sentencing. I didn't receive any visits in this time except for my probation officer. He had to make a report about an appropriate sentence. I never once blamed my troubles on my home life or lack of it, although the authorities were not stupid. No one ever asked how I was, I never offered any information or discussed my emotions, I just had no idea how to. I was very inward and I suppose to a certain extent must have been depressed. I kind of blocked everything out, all I cared about was football, my beloved QPR and the thought of being in the pub drinking loads of lager.

The three weeks went fairly quickly, we spent most of our time in the cell, I read books and if we were lucky enough read a newspaper which had already been read by half the block and was a couple of days old. I read every word in those papers, just to kill time.

The day to go back to court finally arrived; my stomach was full of butterflies, what was going to happen?

When I was in the cell at court, my probation officer showed up and said that my good mate Mikey's Nan had turned up. This was a surprise and a last minute thing. Mikey's Nan was offering to take me in and I would live there. This was like a guardian angel had been sent to rescue me; I would certainly have gone to Youth Custody at Feltham otherwise. My poor old mum was nowhere to be seen, I believe she had been sectioned again and was in Horton Hospital, Epsom, Surrey.

To this day I can't remember the exact sentence I received, I did walk free from the court though, and Mikey's Nan Peggy had been a godsend. What an act of kindness, she was a salt of the earth; she originally came from Notting Hill.

I ended up living with Mikey in his bedroom on a mattress on the floor until they got another single bed. Also in the house was Mikey's mum, step father and brother Nick. We lived in Teddington, back to the town where mum had bought me back to from Australia.

Nick was a bricklayer and I ended up getting a job as a labourer on the building site where he worked. I was paid £85 a week which in 1984 was not too bad.

So for now that was the end of my era living on the farm, Butts Farm.

Mum was in psychiatric hospital more often than not. I hated seeing her in there; it was like one who flew over the cuckoos nest. I hated what mum had become, I was ashamed and embarrassed. I did not want to visit her, it just made me go crazy and I wanted to hurt someone and get involved in fights even more after I had seen her in those places. I am sure no one could understand why I distanced myself from mum, well I never told anyone, and so they could never have known.

Mikey had a new girlfriend, so he was always with her in the evenings; I was a bit gutted as we were close as mates.

I ended up going to the local working men's club round the corner with Nick, we went out nearly every night playing pool and drinking lager. I used to drink Stella which got me drunk a lot quicker. The money I earned as labourer was enough in those days to go out and still pay my keep to Mikey's mum.

I started taking Nick to QPR, mainly the night midweek games as he was busy doing his own things at the weekends. Nick also became a QPR fan, once you went down the Rangers, that's it you were hooked. QPR had a great atmosphere for a small club and back in the 80's as I said before it was all about the clothes and fighting. One particular game against Man United at home, there was a load of trouble. United had a large London following and their firm was known as the Cockney Reds. There were fights breaking out in all parts of the ground, and when the final whistle went, QPR's mob all got together and followed the Cockney Reds down toward Shepherds Bush Green. There was an almighty roar and it all kicked off in the middle of the road. I was right up there amongst it, it was a real buzz for me, and I had no concept of any fear in me.

When it had all calmed down a bit I saw Nick back down the road, he said he could not believe how much bottle I had going into the Cockney Reds, there were a lot of big lumps of lads among them! I think Nick's respect for me had gone up ten fold on that evening.

When I was indoors with my new family, I was so shy and inward, yet when I went out drinking or to football I turned into someone else. It was my arena to show who I was, or even to just let out all the anger, fear and frustration I had inside me.

Nick used to make fun of me indoors, I didn't realize it was only banter; I used to take it to heart. Sometimes in our local pub The Builders Arms he would still take the piss in front of everyone. One night I had had enough and just banged him one straight on the nose. It was quickly broken up; Nick was shocked and did not hit me back. Nick was a strong brickie and older than me so this was a real surprise to everyone.

The day after I hit Nick I went back in the Builders for a few pints, it was opening time and as I sat supping my first pint; in walked Nick with his cousin Graham. Firstly Nick snarled at me "What the fuck are you doing in here?"

After the events last night it was almost as if I should not have shown my face. I had to stand my ground, so I just offered Nick outside to settle things. We both went out the public bar door and stood face to face in the middle of the road. I just had to go with it and do my best. Nick just looked at me and shook my hand; he said fair play he didn't realize I had such a good punch on me.

I explained to Nick that I had enough of him taking the piss and ridiculing me the way he did. Nick said it was just banter, and I told him I did not see it that way. After that Nick stopped mocking me, he still had his moments, but he backed off and there was always a lot of respect given after that.

I had certainly developed a strong self preservation, I could not let anyone walk over me, and I believe that little stint on remand in Latchmere had toughened me right up. And all the shenanigans at football had taken any fear of fighting or being in dangerous situations away from me.

My time living with Mikey and his family was never dull to say the least, although I was very inward and self conscious and had no voice. We got up to all sorts of mischief, and also criminal activity. If I am to be honest all I ever wanted to do was get drunk, the others were more interested in getting drunk and then earning money. We robbed shops and more often than not we were caught. Well I got captured more than the rest as I was always more pissed up then them. It was clothing we were after, as I said the 1980's was all about the casual scene. The clothes were mainly for ourselves but a few quid could be made as they were easy to get rid of. Usually I was the gopher who had to go into the shops first and hence I was also last man out straight into awaiting coppers who had been alerted. We were no criminal masterminds that is for sure.

I was also now right into football violence and again because of my heavy drinking I did not know when to take myself out of a situation. When fights had stopped I would still be in a rage and wanting for the trouble to continue or fight the police when they tried arresting me.

My local magistrate's court was Richmond, and that became my second home. I received various short sentences inside and spent two spells in Detention Centre. The first sentence I got four months and one day which was for assaulting a copper in Chertsey, Surrey. Mikey had a cousin who lived right by Chertsey Bridge, he could have a good fight and there were not many lads I was wary of in those days but Graham sure was tough. A lot of the lads in Chertsey had scooters, either Lambrettas or Vespas. Mikey had a lovely Lambretta; all chromed up with a mural on the side of the Small Faces the band from the 1960's. I never became a Mod but I did start to like the music and I went on a couple of scooter rallies with Mikey, Graham and the boys from Chertsey. There was always trouble with the police at Scooter events, which was right up my street, as I loved the beer and aggro.

Another of my good friends at the time was Tony, he lived in Feltham. Now Tony was one of the most unlucky fellas when it came to fighting. There was a good little gang of us who went together to QPR home and away. This was the era of going away on the service trains; West Ham ICF mob had really started all this using the Persil vouchers for cheaper travel. Poor old Tony had his nose busted at Nottingham Forest away and in another game against Forest at home he had a brand new leather jacket ripped to bits. That was a mad game; it had been snowing heavily and was a night game. For some reason the floodlights went out, this was a cue for the Forest mob that had sneaked into our seats to kick off. We had a good row in the corner of the stand and did well, except Lucky Tony who ended up tumbling down a few seats with his new jacket ripped. I bet he hated the sight of Nottingham Forest.

It was Tony's birthday and we all decide to go to Chertsey, there was a great pub there called the Galleon and a night club by Chertsey Bridge. QPR were playing Birmingham away the next day. We had all arranged to go out have a great night and go back to Tony's in Feltham, get up early and get up to Brum on the train. About 8 of us had got together for this evening and trip. A load of the other's had come out to Chertsey for the evening, Mikey, Graham, the Chertsey boys and a few others from Teddington.

We were having a great evening in the Galleon; it was full of girls, playing some great Jazz Funk tunes and loads of other local lads. As we were mainly

QPR supporters we started singing football songs, that was OK while we were in the Galleon, but as soon as we left we were followed out by a group of about fifteen local lads. It turned out they were from Addlestone and were all Chelsea fans. Needless to say it all kicked off on Chertsey Bridge. The old bill got there very quickly, and everyone managed to get out of there or conveniently vanish. A copper got me from behind as I was the idiot still shouting in the middle of the bridge wanting more. As I was grabbed and heard the "You're nicked" statement I threw my head back and nutted my arresting officer. Tony tried to calm down the situation, he was nicked as well.

I created hell back at Addlestone police station and I was even left in handcuffs in the cell overnight; which I am sure was illegal.

Tony was released and thankfully he was able to meet back up with the boys and they all went to Birmingham in the morning.

I was charged with Actual Bodily Harm to the officer, when I nutted him he apparently had bitten through his tongue. Luckily I got bail, but it was not looking too great.

My drunkenness had started to become very costly

and I never saw this as a problem. I was asked by the magistrate to go for a psychiatric report through the Probation service. I went to Feltham and into a small room, a bit like a doctor's room, behind the desk sat a stern looking man with rounded glasses. This psychiatrist certainly was not the most welcoming man and he didn't even seem to care too much about my predicament. As I have already mentioned I was not the most talkative individual especially around my feelings or anything to do with life whatsoever. I was asked a couple of basic questions about my lifestyle, I probably answered that everything was OK, which really it was not, but what did I know?

I had spoken to someone about having a psychiatric report and they had told me that a lad they knew had been asked to peel an orange football. This seemed bizarre and to be honest I did not believe and thought it was just a bullshit story. But hey presto my friendly shrink asked me to do exactly that, he handed me a full size orange football, the type we used in the playground back at school, the one that bounced like a space hopper.

"I would like to ask you to peel this" he said without a blink and over his rounded focals.

"How can I peel that, it's made of rubber" was my

reply, ha-ha I thought to myself you won't get me. I wondered afterwards what kind of answers other's had given. I bet some lads who wanted to play the system had tried to peel the ball just to appear that they were mad. I did not want to go down that road, so maybe mine was the right response. Anyway I walked out of that room still a sane young man.

During the few weeks waiting for the court case, I managed to get arrested again. We had all been out for the night down the local pub and did our usual crawl along Teddington High Street. There was about eight of us and making the usual noise as we staggered along and over the bridge into Broad Street. At the end or the beginning; depending on which way you saw it was an electrical shop that sold all the latest and modern appliances. In the window this evening was a display of Hoovers, one of the lads made the call to smash the window, "Who's going to bust the window"? Was the cry. And me being the most gullible and drunk as usual proceeded to find a brick and launched it through the air and through the big window. There was a mad rush toward the hoovers, and in no time the shop front was cleared and around half a dozen items were lifted and off with their new owners down the road.

We had a fifteen minute walk back home and by the time we turned our last corner there was a Police van lying in wait. Someone must have heard the commotion and called the law. We tried running into some bushes in someone's front garden and ditched the hoovers, but it was too late we had been seen and were caught red handed.

So here I was sitting in the back of a cop van in handcuffs, this was becoming a regular occurrence, and a lot of the PC's even knew me by name by now.

The charge was Burglary, and to my relief I was out on bail, so I now had two court appearances to worry about. I never really thought too much about it, I would just drown it all out with pints of Stella and have a laugh and joke about it all.

I had left my job as labourer, I can't remember if I was laid off or went by choice. I was now working with a good pal, Joe. Joe and his brother Will had their own window cleaning round in Richmond, a very affluent area. We cleaned the houses of some very well known actors, actresses, MP's and other important figures. Joe had inherited the round from his father who had tragically died. It was all ladder work, Joe was like Spiderman, and he had no fear of heights or danger. He would carry round a big heavy double 15 foot metal ladder and go up three or four stories and walk round ledges. Luckily I was kept on the lower level stuff. But one day we were cleaning a road that had no ground floor windows so I went up to a big bay window, Joe asked me to climb onto the ledge. I must admit I was shitting it a bit, I was shaking, Joe said to hold on to the metal rings that pulled down the sash windows for balance. I jumped up very gingerly and went round the window ledges cleaning the glass. Joe took the ladder away and went round the back of the house, he left me up there for what seemed like half an hour, I kept shouting for him to let me down. When Joe finally came back he was wetting himself with laughter.

"What's so funny, what took you so long?" I asked in my sulking teenager voice.

"That's my way of getting you used to heights Dave"

I thought Joe was taking the piss, but he wasn't and I supposed that was a good way to break me in as a window cleaner.

We used to try and have a good laugh when we were working. Joe invented a game for us to play while we worked and went from house to house.

Richmond was full of rich people and had a lot of shops and offices around the town. There certainly were a lot of nice looking women around! To amuse ourselves, every time we passed a girl or woman we would give her a rating of one to three, this passed our time and made the day seem not so boring. I worked on and off over the years with Joe, his brother Will got banged up for a while so when there were just two of us we seemed to have more of a laugh. In fact at some stage we all spent little spells inside for some weekend stupidity.

My turn for a stint in nick came round sooner than I had hoped. I was still on bail for the incident with the copper in Chertsey and the shop burglary.

I went to Chertsey magistrate's court and pleaded guilty to the charge of Actual Bodily Harm to the PC. I was sentenced to three months Detention Centre. I was taken in a van by two screws (prison officers) and the driver. We did not pick anyone else up along the way. I was going to Aldington DC in Kent, fairly near Ashford. This was an ex Prisoner of War camp from WW2 apparently and was in the middle of fields full of sheep. It was surrounded by high wire fencing with customary razor wire for good measure. One of the screws in the van seemed fairly decent and gave me a kind warning that as soon as I got out the van to run as fast as I could when asked by the awaiting officer.

True to his word when the vans doors opened up on the massive courtyard, that looked like what you see in films for military parades and all the marching etc.

"Casellas, go through that door and when I say go, you look straight forward and no turning back" this was the command from the immaculate looking officer, he reminded me of someone from the Gestapo.

I legged it and went through the door that I was shown and in to the reception area. This was a bit similar to Latchmere, the time I had been on remand before. Although the atmosphere and hospitality was much more cold and stricter. All of the usual questions and details were taken and then I was asked to strip off and make my way to another small desk in the corner. Another screw was waiting there and had a big ink pad open and ready for me to give my fingerprints. The amount of times I had already done this at Twickenham police station, I just had to go with it and follow orders.

Once my prints were taken, I was marched into what was a bathroom, it was sparse with just an empty bath and a stiff white towel hanging on it's own by the door.

"Right Casellas, fill that bath up with cold water and wash yourself, you have three minutes to get clean and leave the bath as you found it" Already I hated this place with a vengeance.

The big problem was I still had ink smothered all over my hands and trying to wash myself in cold water was no walk in the park. I had to empty the bath and it was covered in inky smears, all over the taps and cast iron surround. Three minutes is not a long time to deal with the requested task. I just about made it otherwise I would have been slapped about.

Still naked from the inky bath, I was given a box full of prison uniform and bedding. I was marched army style by my S.S officer straight down a long corridor and into a dimly lit dormitory. It must have gone 8pm by now and there were rows of beds opposite each other and each bed had an inmate in it. It was silent, and all I could feel was around thirty pairs of eyes on me, talk about being self conscious!

The prison uniform that I had been issued had a number stamped on it, and to this day I remember mine was number 24. My prison number was

D94860, I had many different numbers over the years but this one stuck with me forever. The reason I cannot forget that number was because every morning we had to bark our prison number to the screw waiting at the washroom, we were given a nasty metal razor and told to shave whether we needed to or not. And we had to use prison issue soap which stung like hell on our face; we also had our own shaving brush to lather up the soap. It was medieval, I saw some lads with blood pouring from nicks on their skin from the razors. A few times I cut myself as well. When we done shaving and cleaning our teeth, with powdered toothpaste we then had to hold our hands out and show our finger nails. They had to be cut or another slap was given. And this was just the start to the day, with many more delights to follow!

The food in Aldington was healthy enough, we ate a lot of home grown salad and I must admit I enjoyed the coleslaw made by inmates. Everyone had to work in there; I worked in a shop floor which made toy tractors. I had to put the wheels on them, and boy my fingers were raw as it was no easy task. There was another workshop with the old fashioned Looms which made prison blankets, I was glad I was not put on that as it looked like serious graft.

There were two screws in the tractor shop; Fuck-up and Lofty, they were famous throughout the prison community everyone had heard of them. Fuck-up got his name literally because he would fuck you up if you did anything out of line. Lofty was just a tall gangly bloke that reminded me of Mr Mackay in Porridge. They were super strict to say the least. If anyone ever wanted to go to the toilet we had to ask for toilet paper. Fuck-up would hand over just five sheets of the thinnest paper you could possibly get. His reasoning for five sheets; you use "2 up, 2 down and one for a polish"! Luckily we were eating healthy food because if anyone got the runs, imagine only having five sheets to clean up with.

In the evenings there would be an hour of education and an hour of association. Association was everyone's favourite time, because the TV would be on, there was also Pool, cards and other games we could play.

During the day there would be one hour of Physical Training that was brutal. It was taken by an ex Royal Marine who was now a prison instructor. I saw a couple of lads in tears because the sessions were so hard. We were not allowed to smoke in DC and I had never been so fit in my life. At the weekends we were able to play football or rugby. One weekend I played in the rugby team for us inmates versus the screws. This was our chance to get a few sly digs in!

The DC was run like an army camp but maybe a bit more brutal, Detention Centres were soon to be banned for reports and evidence of its harsh brutality.

The day came when I was to be released; only I was not let out as I had the other pending case for the shop burglary. I was gutted I had to go on remand, and I was taken in a van to Lewes prison in Sussex. Lewes was a nasty looking place it was built into what looked like rock. There were two wings there for Juveniles, one remand and one for convicted cons. The day I got there I was put in the old Napoleonic wing and in a cell with a black fella we shared a bunk bed. I forgot to mention that I had my head shaved down to the bone at Aldington, as every inmate had to.

While I was in the cell a load of black lads came to the door and peered through the spy hole.

"Oi skinhead you're a dead man" was shouted through the door. The lads must have made the assumption that I was racist because of my shaved head. How was I going to get out of this shit?

When we were let out for evening tea, I was on my guard as I thought I was going to be steamed by the lads who came to my door. Luckily nothing happened but I did request to see the senior officer.

I explained my situation and asked if there was any chance of being transferred somewhere nearer home. Mikey was on remand in Ashford, Middlesex for the shop burglary, the same charge I was being held for.

I went back to my cell and about an hour later the door opened and one of the screws told me to get my kit together. If there was a God, I was being looked after because I was told there was a van leaving for Ashford, and I was going on it!

To say I was relieved to get out of there was an understatement and I was going to be in the same nick as my pal Mikey, happy days!

Ashford was another prison similar to Latchmere House in it's layout except it was much bigger. The blocks were three stories and had long landings with separate staircases, not like the big open wings on the old Victorian prisons. While I was there I witnessed a lot of taxing, and that occurred on the staircases, small gangs would wait by the doorway and rob lads coming back from visits. In those days when on remand, visitors could bring in food, drinks and other bits and pieces. After a visit all the goods were put in a plastic tray, and as you walked back to the landing, this was when people were ambushed and taxed for their goodies. Again, luckily enough I was never robbed myself, but came very near to it. I know I would never let anyone just take my stuff; I would rather take a kicking than just get mugged off like that.

There was another lad Eddie on remand, he lived literally round the corner from myself and Mikey in Teddington. I ended up sharing a cell with him and Mikey was next door. Eddie was always joking around; we decided to play a trick on Mikey one night. To get stuff to your neighbour a line was made up of ripped sheets and stuff tied on to the end. The line was then swung back and forth through the open barred window. If you got caught, there would be a punishment of having privileges taken away. We never got caught thankfully.

Eddie asked Mikey through the window would he like some chocolate; of course he said yes. Eddie was a sick fucker; he had shit in a newspaper and rolled it up to make a little parcel. This was put in a bag and Eddie swung it across to Mikey.

We waited in anticipation; "You dirty bastards",

Mikey roared and myself and Eddie almost fell on the floor laughing. To be honest I thought this prank was a bit over the top, but went along with it anyway.

We had some good laughs in the weeks on remand, but it was no bed of roses. Eddie had already been to court and sentenced by the time we were due up.

Myself and Mikey appeared back at Richmond Magistrates, my second home. For the charge of shop burglary we both got the maximum detention centre sentence; four months and one day. I have no idea what the one day bit was all about!

Guess where we went? Yep back to Aldington where I had only been just those several weeks ago.

Now Mikey had been on remand in Ashford for a few months so his time was served and he was going to be released in two days the lucky fucker. Because I had served the three month sentence for the ABH on Police, I had a fair bit of this new sentence to complete.

This time when we arrived at Aldington, I was more prepared for what was to come at reception. I had briefed Mikey at what to expect. Mikey was out the van first and he legged it to the door leading into the Gestapo's welcoming area.

My turn and I was asked to run like the wind into reception. As I entered the door I was slapped hard round the face by one of the men in black.

"Back again Casellas, wasn't your time here before not tough enough for you?" This wasn't a question, more of a gloating statement from Hitler's apprentice.

It was the same procedure, head shaved, inky bath etc etc. I was first back into the dorm. And Mikey soon followed naked in all his glory minus his hair!

Mikey was put in the bed next to me, we were not allowed to talk, but I could not stop laughing hysterically. I thought it was hilarious that Mikey had his head shaved and was being released in two days, you would of thought they would of let him off having his barnet destroyed like that.

The day Mikey left, I was absolutely gutted; I soon got over it though, I had to.

4 MARCHING ON TO WEMBLEY

When I was finally released from Aldington, I was fit as a fiddle. I was given a week's dole money in cash when I was sent out the door. A prison van took us to the train station, and as soon as I arrived I went straight to the newsagents and bought a packet of cigarettes. I was with one other lad who had been released with me, he told me his parents were going to be waiting for him back at Waterloo. There was going to be no one waiting for me, but I was going straight back to Mikey's and we were all going to go out that night.

Once on the train, and we had pulled off on our journey back into freedom. What a great feeling this was, but I still had not given a thought for my mum. All I could think about was getting pissed and so I went straight to the trains buffet bar and bought four cans of my favourite. The lad with me did not want to drink so early in the morning but I kind of twisted his arm and he had no choice but to join me.

The Stella hit me quickly, as it did for my new drinking buddy; we were both half drunk as we arrived back at the good old smoky Capital, London Town.

I always wondered what kind of reception the lad got from his parents, he kept telling me he did not drink, yet I had strong armed him into get lashed up with me.

I made it back to Teddington, settled back in with Mikey's family and we all went out that night to the pubs in Hampton Court. I was buzzing to be free again and we all got well drunk that night and ended up in a fight with some other lads. This was just the norm for the 1980's, if we didn't get a row with other lads we would end up rucking the local bouncers who were always up for it.

There was a night club on the side of the Clarence hotel in Teddington and every Friday there would be a big group of us, and come chucking out time we would always resist leaving the gaff; we did not want our night to end. There was a big built tall bouncer, who loved getting involved with us, one night he took a right hammering with lumps of wood and boots to the head. Even though he had taken such a beating, he was back on the door the following weekend, so respect to him for that.

For some reason in my own mind I felt I never really belonged with Mikey's family. I was made very welcome and never judged for any of my actions, the boys were no saints either. But I was very inward and shy believe it or not and always felt very self conscious and inferior. I was probably depressed about my mum's mental problems but never could show or talk about that.

My life consisted of working, I had various jobs; going out as many nights I could afford and going to QPR home and away as much as I could. I was always being arrested for something, mainly drunken fighting or stupid shop burglaries. The burglaries were mainly being in the company of others, and I just went along with it. The clothes and any money came in handy, but I was never the sort who planned criminal activity; I was just an angry teenager really who loved fighting.

When I turned 18 years old I decided I wanted to go back and live in Mum's flat at Butts Farm. Probably not the best move, the flat had deteriorated and smelled of piss. Someone had been sleeping in my little room, and all the carpets were filthy and basically the place was just a hovel. I put up with it though and managed to get rid of the drunks who had been staying there.

The only thing that really kept me going was football; it was my escape as was the booze. In 1986 QPR had a great run in the League Cup which was then known as the Milk Cup. We got to the quarter final and played our hated neighbours Chelsea at home. The first game was a draw. Chelsea in the 1980's had one of the best hooligan mobs in the country they were notorious. However they were bully boys when it came to playing us, they would outnumber QPR and from the 1960's would take over our ground when we played them. It was around this era that we started to fight back a bit. The night we played Chelsea all I wanted to do was hit as many Chelsea lads as I could get away with! I did just that and did get away with it.

The replay was a midweek game at Stamford Bridge, this was well before the Bridge had been modernized and the away end was a curved crumbling terrace that even had weeds growing out the cracks in the concrete. The view was well away from the pitch but it had that great atmosphere of old school football grounds in those days. That night the rain poured down and the pitch almost became a pool of water. We won 2-0 and one of our goals was scored from almost the halfway line; all the QPR fans went berserk behind that goal. It was such a great feeling beating our enemies like that, I did not personally get involved in any trouble after the game and went straight home as I had work in the morning.

We were drawn against the mighty Liverpool in the semi-final, in those days the League cup semi was a two legged affair. We won the first leg at home 1-0, what a great result.

When I went to QPR I spent a lot of time in the Goldhawk pub which was obviously down Goldhawk Road in Shepherds Bush. The landlord of the Goldhawk was Irish and most of the punters in there were Irish or second generation Irish. There was a micky taking nickname for second generation, Plastic Paddies they were called! A lot of my pals were of Irish descent, and my good mate Tony from Feltham also knocked about in there with this lot.

The lads in the Goldhawk decided to take two coaches to Liverpool, and there were many other coaches from all over the place going as well. The coach left early so we got up there before pub opening time. The coach parked in the car park of the infamous Stanley Park, which kind of separated Liverpool from Everton's grounds.

Everyone was drinking on the coach from the off and the atmosphere was buzzing. We all took a stroll round the local area, to be fair it was quite dead, not a lot of people about. We headed into an off licence before the pubs opened, and what struck me at the time was that the counter was divided by glass screens with just an small opening to pay the fella and receive your goods. These screens had not even been introduced to London yet, that is how rough Liverpool was back in those days. After a few cans and milling around we found a pub that was open, called The Arkle, probably named after the famous racehorse that won the Grand National.

More and more QPR fans arrived and now the Arkle was heaving with every face from QPR. There was a good three of four hundred of us in that boozer, and everyone was in very high spirits. As we neared to kick off time, about an hour or so before; in walked a few young scouse lads known as Scallies. It was obvious they had been sent by their elders to see who and how many of us QPR were in there. They left sharpish, and now the atmosphere started to change. All the talk was that Liverpool's firm would be back soon; no way would they stand for one of their pubs being taken like this. The feelings were of tense excitement, I always felt that sensation on my stomach when I knew something was going to happen. It was a sense of danger, and also a buzz at the same time. There was a shout from the entrance door; "They're here". Everyone ran to get outside and true to what we thought about the scallies, they had directed their mob to us.

Outside it was kicking off everywhere, and of course I wanted to get involved. In 1986 the fashion had turned a bit toward wearing Ski Wear, jackets with hoods. I pulled up my hood over my face, mainly because it was freezing outside and I also didn't want my face slashed with a Stanley knife. Scousers were a bit notorious for cutting people with knives, and Stanley Park was an ironic name as a lot of lads got ambushed in there.

I was in the middle of the road by now and started to trade blows with one of my counterparts, everyone started running and going back in the pub. I was raged up and well drunk by now, so I just carried on trying to kick the scouse lad as he ran off. What I did not see was the coppers had arrived from behind us with their truncheons drawn. I was wrestled to the ground and stuck in handcuffs...

again! Yep Davy boy has managed to get himself arrested again, my problem was I did not gauge danger or even have the awareness to see around me, I just waded in fighting, because that was my release and excitement.

I was taken to the Police station in Walton, which was over by Everton's ground. I was gutted, I had come all this way and was going to miss one of QPR's biggest matches in our history.

All the usual procedure of handing in belongings, name giving, fingerprints taken and then slammed in a cell. All I could think about was having another beer and getting to the game. When was I going to be let out, how would I get home? I had told the police I had came up on a coach and did not have the funds to get a train home.

It was my lucky night, a typical scouse looking copper complete with moustache opened up the door and told me I was being released. I had to sign bail papers and return in a couple of weeks to go to court.

"We're giving you a chance to go watch the second half lad" explained the desk sergeant. "And make sure you stay out of trouble, or things can only get worse"

I asked for directions to Anfield and walked sharply, it was easy enough to spot the brightly lit floodlights and the noise of the crowd.

As I made my way in and up the stairs to the away section there was a roar, QPR had scored and made it 1-1. The R's fans were going ballistic. The atmosphere in that end that night was mental we drew the game 2-2, both of our goals were own goals from the scousers, we were in the final!

Dad worked at The Sun Newspaper, being an Aussie he knew Rupert Murdoch and was a sub editor for the sports news. My old man managed to get me three tickets for the Milk Cup Final at Wembley. QPR were to play Oxford United; our manager was Jim Smith who used to be the boss and was much loved at Oxford. We had beaten Chelsea and Liverpool, surely the cup was ours!

QPR fans had a good old tradition of walking en masse to Wembley from our ground in Shepherds Bush. This started when we got to the League Cup Final in 1967, and again in 1982 when we played Spurs in the FA Cup Final. Myself Mart and a load of others all joined the march in 1982, great day and of course all pissed up on cider.

This was 1986; I was older and always involved in

aggro at football. I was full of excitement as usual on match day and had the added bonus of being able to sell the two extra tickets that Dad had got me.

All our usual suspects met up at the Bush and we walked up past the Scrubs and onto Willesden Junction. Wembley was not too many miles away from QPR and all the off licences took a bit of a battering along the way. We got within a mile of the ground and settled in a pub which I can never remember the name of.

Being a Wembley final and we had probably around 40.000 fans that were going and there were different mobs all over the place. Mart wasn't with me that day; I ended up getting paralytic as usual and still hadn't got rid of my two spare tickets. My plan was to sell them outside the stadium; there would always be plenty of fans needing a ticket.

Around 30 of us all left together and made our way to the twin towers. As we approached the majestic arena scuffles were breaking out with Oxford fans. I ran in ready to do battle with whoever wanted it, and what I saw next was quite shocking. A lad from Oxford got a full bottle whacked round the side of his face and blood poured out all over the place. Even our lot thought this well out of order and the

QPR fella that did it received a volley of abuse and a good smack on the nose for good measure.

The law rushed in and guess who got lifted? Yes me again, and no word of a lie I was bundled up between two mounted policeman and literally carted off with my legs in the air. My feet did not touch the ground until we arrived at one of the vast car parks around the stadium. There were two sweat boxes parked up and obviously filling up with prisoners, there had been quite a lot of trouble throughout the build-up to the match.

So here I was again, sat in a tiny cubicle when I should have been selling the two tickets and getting into the ground ready for one of QPR's biggest matches in our history.

We must have been stuck in this car park up until half time, a good forty five minutes. I heard a roar and was so convinced we had scored, I let out a roar. One of the coppers in the van sneered and told me it was Oxford who had scored. Could this day get any worse?

QPR lost the game 3-0, and apparently were not even in the contest at all. What a let down, and to rub salt in the wound I got a £350 fine at Willesden Magistrates, and all for being a dickhead.

Life carried on, Mum was still in and out of mental wards, and I was working, drinking and fighting at football and in the pubs. That was it in a nutshell. I hardly saw Dad; he had probably disowned me by now for all the trouble I was getting in.

At the end of 1986 I was losing control, fighting just for the sake of it in and outside the local pubs. It was almost as if I became the entertainment for everyone, or that's how it seemed. My mate Joe, the window cleaner was also a complete loon and one night we ended up having a big ruck with a load of off duty coppers drinking in Hampton Wick. Yes we got nicked and for once we were just chucked out the station in the morning.

Then came Southampton away, I went with the boys from Feltham in one of the lads motors. Tony was with us, out of all my mates he was definitely the most sensible. He would try and talk some sense to me, but it always fell on deaf ears. We lost the game as usual and the usual mob I knocked about with at football were there. Everyone had the hump that we lost and the talk was everyone was going to march into town and kick off with Southampton, if we could find them. I told Tony I was going with the lads, he tried his hardest for me to see reason and go back in the car with them. Of course I did not listen or take his advice.

There were only about 25 of us who got it together and go into the town centre. There were a couple of young lads with us and they were sent ahead on a mission to see if there was a firm of Southampton about. We all waited, buzzing for it by a big roundabout not too far from the rail station.

All of a sudden the boys came running back; "There's fucking loads of em" shouted one of our scouts and well out of breath.

About ten seconds behind them came a charge of about 60 of Southampton's finest. What struck me first was that their lad at front was shouting and had a scouse accent. Southampton is one of the biggest docks in the UK, and a lot of dockers came from Liverpool.

We were outnumbered by more than two to one; this didn't usually bother me, but one of our lot made a decision; "Let's get back up on top of that railway bridge and hold em off there".

That seemed a good idea; we all retreated and stood firm at the top of the small narrow footbridge over the railway tracks.

Southampton kept going past and over toward the

station, we decided to go back through the station from the other side of the tracks and out onto the entrance.

We all stood in the forecourt of the station, and bottles started flying back and forth and smashing on the ground everywhere. There was one lone copper in the middle of us all trying to quell the baying mobs. He had no chance, my mate Alex went to kick an oncoming Saint and he slipped over straight on his arse, I tried to shield him from the further onslaught. Then in a flash a Chinese lad came flying through the air Kung Fu style straight for my head. I put my arm up and he connected with force. A few more punches were traded between the two groups and then the sound of sirens and the screeching of the tyres on several police vans.

Everyone dispersed quickly, and for once I went with them instead of carrying it on and getting nicked. We all made it back to the platform, everyone was hyper but still trying to look innocent at the same time. Thankfully no one was arrested. All the talk was of how well we had done to stand our ground with all the odds against us.

A train pulled in but it wasn't ours, a mob of around thirty blokes got off; "Here we go again" someone commented.

The usual "Who are you lot?" came from their boy at the front. It turned out they were Bristol Rovers coming back from Portsmouth or somewhere. We told them we had just had it with Southampton and they were keen to team up with us and go back into town for some more. Everyone had had enough and wanted to get on the next train back to London. But we paid our respect to the Rovers lads and made our way back to the smoke and our nights out.

I ended up going back to the Royal Oak in Teddington, this was where all my mates went these days.

I told everyone all about the day's events at football and carried on drinking loads of pints. My arm was in a lot of pain by now, and I kept moaning on about it.

Eventually someone offered to take me to hospital, and for once I did the right thing and went instead of continuing to get bladdered.

It turned out my arm was broken, and it was put in plaster. What a bummer, this still would not interfere with my drinking though!

A week or two later we was all out at the Royal Oak

again and by the end of the night things were getting very lively as usual. Mum used to bring back various men from the pub before we ended up at Butts Farm. The only fella I really liked was Jim, he was second generation Irish and originally from Acton. He respected mum and took a shine to me.

Jim was a hardcore drinker just like me and most of our group; we always ended up well pissed and up to some kind of no good. This particular night police were called to the pub, and it all got heated outside. Jim ended up getting nicked; as they carted him off to the awaiting van I was having none of it.

Even though my arm was in plaster I stepped in and smashed one of the PC's round the side of his head. I ended up face down on the pavement with my arms up by back and handcuffed again. When would I ever learn?

Myself and Jim spent the weekend in the cells and taken to Richmond Magistrates on the Monday morning. We were both remanded in custody. I had already been inside for assaulting the old bill, so it was not looking too great for me to say the least.

When we were taken to Lambeth holding cells, I gave a false date of birth. I wanted to stay with Jim and go to adult prison. My ruse worked and we both were delivered to Brixton Prison. That first night we shared a cell, what a crazy scenario.

When the morning came, the big heavy iron door swung open, and a perplexed looking screw stood there staring at me.

"Casellas you little shit, we've got your real date of birth"

"Shit" I thought to myself, I was going to Feltham.

"A coach is leaving for Chelmsford, and you are on it" I was told.

I don't know what God is up there but I was saved from going to Feltham yet again.

Chelmsford was an adult prison, but it had two wings for Young prisoners. One was for convicted inmates and one for those on remand. I wrote to my Dad and he came up to visit me. This was the first time Dad had really shown any concern or interest in what was going on in my life. Dad said he would try and send me to live with my Gran in Australia to start a new life.

I really did not want to leave England; I had too many mates here and of course my beloved QPR. Dad said he would come to court and explain to the judge to let me off if I pledged to start again in the Land of Oz I was to be sentenced in Crown Court which probably meant I was going to get a stiff term of imprisonment.

After three weeks on remand, I was up at Kingston Crown Court for sentencing. Dad was there in a smart suit and he stood in the dock and pleaded with the Judge to agree to our plan. The judge did agree and bailed me for a month, and insisted that we return with a single air ticket to Perth, Australia to prove I was going.

Would you Adam and Eve it! This was like I was being deported out of England as a criminal; just like all those years ago with the prison ships and first settlers in Oz.

Even though I was born in Australia, I never felt I belonged there, my heart was in London and I was gutted.

I did love my time living with Dad for that month. Even though he was at work from lunchtime right through to the next morning, I hardly saw Dad. But Dad's home was spotless, he had a cleaner come in every few days. Lynn his second wife was at work during the day and I was unemployed; but only because of my pending situation.

All my best pals were also upset I was going to live 12.000 miles away. We had a good old leaving do at one of the pubs in Teddington. And to be honest there was a few tears shed. Tony from Feltham arranged a stripogram who pretended to be a WPC.

So there I was a modern day convict, going to sunnier climates to start a new life.

5 AUSTRALIA'S LAST CONVICT

The total journey time to Perth, Australia was thirty two hours; that included a one hour stop in Bahrain and six hours at Hong Kong.

I knew myself that I could not be trusted to leave the airport at Hong Kong, which we had the option to do.

If I had of gone out to explore the bars I was sure that I would have missed my flight. So I sat at the bar in the terminal and got hammered. I ended up having a good chat with another Aussie; we spoke about football and other bloke things.

The airline I flew with was Cathay Pacific, the stewardesses were well nice and the food was also top notch. I did not see any of that on the last leg of the flight from Hong Kong to Perth; around ten hours.

I got so drunk at the airport that I don't even remember taking off, I woke up a dribbling mess as the captain was announcing that we were circling Perth airport! Sitting next to me were two very fit looking Aussie girls, what must I have looked like?!

I was still wearing a tracksuit hoody, totally the wrong attire for Oz, my new home. What struck me as I went down the escalators and out into the forecourt was that the heat hit me like opening an oven door. And it was dark and about 10pm, when I had left England, it was still very cold, my lack of research and awareness of different climates was non existent.

I was met by my Uncle Paul, and his family. They welcomed me and they even commented on why I was wearing a hooded track top. We drove through the city of Perth, and they showed me the Casino and other landmarks. It was all very exciting, but at the same time I already missed all my mates.

Paul dropped me off at my Grandmother's house, she was so kind and seemed genuinely happy to see me and put me up. No one ever really mentioned all the trouble I had been in, except my two young cousins, Paul's sons. They were infatuated by it all and seemed proud that I was a bit of a fighter.

Gran said she would cook me a breakfast every morning and an evening meal. She even stocked up on cans of lager and I was to be allowed four "tinnies" a night. This was paradise, what more could I want? The Aussies have a big drinking culture, so I was certainly in the right place.

The second day I was there, I went out in the back garden and sat there in my shorts and took off my top. Being English, I had to soak up as much sun when it was there. The sun was here alright, it was fierce. Nan warned me to only leave my top off for twenty minutes and cover up with UV protection. I did not listen, I never listened to anyone about anything!

There were Parrots flying around in the garden, multicoloured ones that you only saw in pet shops. I asked Gran were these birds her pets. She laughed loudly and said; "No Dave there are thousands around here:. Parrots were as common as pigeons in this part of the world!

I asked Gran how to get to the city of Perth, it was about a twenty minute drive on the bus. My first thoughts were to go to the pubs and see what they were like. Aussie pubs were all stainless steel and no women. The lager was served in small glasses but the beer was ice cold.

Just for a change I got really pissed on my first venture out. It was dark when I returned and I could not for the life of me remember what bus stop to get off, or remember where Gran lived. I staggered around drunk as a skunk for ages looking for Gran's house.

The next morning Gran was nice about it all, she gave me a bit of a telling off for getting sun burned, I was red raw. She did not mention about me drinking too much though, but reminded me that I had my four can ration.

Back in England I had learned how to do Painting and Decorating; twice at court I had received Community Service Orders and had been made to paint an old people's home and a Salvation Army hut.

I did a few small painting jobs to earn some money; back in the 1980's Australia was so much cheaper to live in than England. Rent was affordable, even when I had to go on the dole, I could live and eat well. Gran never asked for any money from me, but I ended up sharing a ground floor apartment with my cousin Anthony. He worked as a waiter and barman at the time and had a really nice Ford Falcon car. This was like a bigger version of the Ford Granada and was automatic.

I decided it was time to get a drivers licence, I was 19 years old and everyone in Oz seemed to be driving by the legal age of 17.

The apartment I shared with my cousin was a stones throw away from one of the best beaches in the Perth area, Scarborough beach.

Anthony was well into windsurfing, I could see the attraction but it sure wasn't for the feint hearted.

There was this day when we were both not working and it was blowing a gale outside.

"Time to get the board on the roof-rack and down the beach" Anthony announced excitedly.

I went with him, if just to watch and see how he jumped the waves on his board.

It really was super windy and the waves were like mountains. There was no way I would ever have diced with the power of the ocean like Anthony was.

Anthony stayed on the board and was almost flying in the air, and in no time he had vanished out into the horizon. I thought to myself that seemed too far and was all getting a bit dodgy out there.

I started to worry and ran along the beach to see if I

could locate him coming back in to shore. I must have jogged a good half a mile before I saw Anthony's board lying there in the sand. But there was no sign of the rider, my cousin. Now I was thinking that he had drowned or been washed out to sea. There were sharks all round the coast of Western Australia, had he been munched for lunch by a Great White?!

Finally after a few more minutes of heading up the beach, there he was; Anthony was lying face down in the sand like a washed up seal in his black oil skins.

"Shit, I thought you were a gonner" I told Anthony.

He breathlessly replied that he had been caught in a swell. A swell was like a massive undercurrent that takes you down under the sea and spits you back out again.

Anthony agreed and thought his time was up as well. The mad thing is this incident never stopped him from going out again on his board.

Being English and living in Australia, I had to endure comments of being a Pommy bastard almost on a daily basis. I reckoned it was just banter but there were a few that really had a chip on their shoulder.

As I was only 19 years old, and still wet behind the ears, being called a Pom used to piss me off.

I saw an ad in a local newspaper looking for a goalkeeper for a football team in the city of Perth. The Aussies called football, soccer. Their game was Aussie Rules Football. My dad had been a pro in the late 50s early 60s until he had to retire early through injury. So when I asked any of my family would they come and watch me play, they would laugh and say it was a "poofs" game.

The team I played for was Perth Inter, named after Inter Milan and we even wore the same kits as the Italian side. The manager was Sergio, and most of the players were Italian. The Aussies called the Italians "Dings". They had a nickname for everything and everyone. The rest of the squad was made up of a Swede, a German, a Frenchman and about three Aussies. We had a first team and a reserve team. They thought I was such a good keeper that I played for both teams one after another. It was either that, or there was a severe shortage of keepers in our area.

The standard of football was fairly decent, probably about the level of Hayes or Fisher Athletic or lower non-league standard in England.

There was one match we played another Italian based side on midweek under lights scenario. There was a little side stand, and there was a good fifty to a hundred local lads all getting very vocal.

I made a real bad howler in the first few minutes and we ended up getting torn a new one 8-0. This was the worse ever defeat while I was at the club.

We had a winger who was a bit hot-headed himself, and he was being ribbed for being a bit overweight. He lost the plot and ran into the stand and started having a ruck with their army of piss-takers. He was sent off immediately. That was a night to forget, but still sticks in my memory forever!

Anthony took me out one night and we went to a nightclub called "The Underground". There was a lot of Italians who went in there, John Travolta, Saturday Night Fever lookalikes complete with open shirt and gold medallions hanging round their necks.

As I was such a big drinker, I never really had much luck with women. But one night early on before I got too pissed, we ended up chatting to two girls. We both pulled, happy days! Now ironically the girl I met was born in Nottingham and had come to live in Oz when she was very young, which was the same as my history only in reverse. So there we had something in common straight away.

My new girlfriend agreed to come and watch me play in goal for Inter, I was well chuffed.

My middle name certainly was not "Lucky", and that first match I had my new fan was a disaster. I went out to catch a high cross that came over; and the ball hit my thumb straight on and dislocated it quite badly. My thumb was hanging out of its socket upside down. What a nightmare!

My girl in shining armour took me to hospital and the thumb was put back in place. I was not to play football again for at least six weeks.

Every now and then I would phone my mates back in London. I received a massive shock when Mart told me that I could be a father. I had lived with a very kind family for a while, both the daughters had been at my junior school and the girl in my class, I had apparently made pregnant. I was not so sure, but this had really got in my head and I was now starting to get even more homesick than I already was. My girlfriend here in Oz had given me a tape of the latest tunes recorded live in a Nottingham nightclub. I listened to this all morose and sentimental nearly every night.

Another night when Anthony had gone out, I was stuck in and had run out of booze. The bottle shop, which was the Aussie name for an off licence was only a ten minute walk up the road. But I felt really lazy and wanted to take the Ford Falcon for a spin. I had already had a good few cans and half cut already. I got in the car which was parked tightly next to the neighbours motor and hit the accelerator in reverse gear. The car jolted backwards and scraped up the side of the other car. I panicked and parked back up and didn't say a word about the accident to anyone.

In the last couple of weeks I had rang Dad and told him I was really home sick and wanted to come back. He tried to drum it into my head to stay and give it at least a year; I had only been here in Perth for six months.

Eventually I convinced Dad to get me home, he was not at all happy about the situation. Dad sent the money for me to get an airline ticket. Dad said I could come back and live with him until I found a job and then I'd have to go my own way.

I wasn't at Dad's long and ended up living with my alleged baby daughter, her mother and family. Mart had been with the sister for years already, so we were like one big happy family. We were living on a council estate in Teddington and loads of our mates all lived there.

6 THE YOUNG ONES

I got myself a job as a driver's assistant for a firm that delivered real ales and imported bottle lagers to pubs all round the south of England.

This was an ideal job for me as we were often offered drinks by the landlords and helped ourselves to bottles which we put down as breakages.

My mum was out at the time and still living at Butts Farm, social services were in the process of getting her a flat away from the madness of the estate.

I did have a connection with the baby but was never 100% sure she was mine. I arranged to meet my mum at the Builders Arms one Sunday and I was taking the baby in a pram with me. When mum took one look at the girl, she said "that baby is not yours!"

I disagreed as I kind of wanted her to be mine, but mum told me in no uncertain terms that she knew best as she was my mother!

It wasn't long before I found somewhere else to live. I ended up moving into a little room above a video shop just over the road from where I had been living. It was shared with an old school mate and the other lad is the well known Chelsea hooligan who was stitched up on TV by a Mr McIntyre.

If anyone has seen the TV sitcom The Young Ones, then our living conditions were very similar. Jason's sink had been blocked with puke for weeks and someone else had thrown up on the old carpet. Instead of cleaning it up, we cut the piece of carpet that had been puked on with a Stanley knife and threw it out of the window.

We were proper bachelors running riot, and to be honest the place was more like a squat.

I had a bit more contact with my sister now for the first time in years since she was fostered.

Fran worked at a bakers in Twickenham and most nights she would bring cakes and offered to do my washing for me.

Against my religion, I ended up going to watch Chelsea with Jason a few times, but only because of the potential trouble that I loved participating in. I went with him to the home games against West Ham and Millwall. This would have been in 1988 or 89. Both times from what I saw, both the ICF and Millwall took a bit of a liberty at Stamford Bridge. And we did not get in any action whatsoever.

Dad set me up with an interview with the Sun newspaper at Wapping in East London. Dad said all I had to do was turn up and the job was mine. It was a case of who you know, not what you know. The job would have been loading the vans with newspapers through the early hours. If I knuckled down for six months or so, I would have been offered to learn to become a journo.

The night before the interview I went to the pub as usual and got hammered. I did not attend the interview, maybe the worse mistake I ever made in my life. At the time it did not bother me too much as all I cared about was football, mates and pubs.

Another night I was out with Jason, and on the way home we went to get some chips from the chippy up the road. On our way to the chip shop, there were a few girls at a bus stop. I was so pissed, to this day I can't remember if I had said something to them. I could be a proper dick-head at times and I often ended up in aggro as was the norm.

By the time we got our chips and started walking back to the flat along the road something must have been planned.

To get to our flat above the shop, we had to go round the back of some garages and up a rear fire escape into a back door and up the stairs. All I remember is as we turned the corner round the garages; a fist came toward me and must have knocked me straight to the ground. I awoke in a pool of blood in the middle of the road with three coppers standing over me. There was no sign of Jason.

My nose was over the other side of my face and I was a right mess. The PC asked me did I recognize any of the attackers, I told him I was out cold and would find the fuckers myself. I was advised not to do that!

I discharged myself out of hospital that morning and went straight back to the flat. I asked Jason what the fuck had happened, he told me that three white South Africans had jumped us and he admitted to being on his toes, there was nothing he could do.

An old school mate lived across the road and his mum had come out and waned off the slags that had beaten me. She told them she had called the police and they shot off into the night. I was told that the three fuckers, all the size of professional rugby players had been kicking my head like a rag doll while I was on the deck. Maybe I was lucky to be alive.

I had to have an operation on my nose shortly after and to be honest that was the worse pain I have ever experienced. When I woke up from the op, I was in a recovery room with a load of other patients. It was like a scene from MASH, the comedy about the US military field hospital.

The surgeons had to drill a new nostril for me as my nose had been blocked with smashed bone and I could not breathe. Even to this day I still cannot breathe 100% and still get headaches.

This beating still did not deter me from getting drunk and continuing my lifestyle. I still went to football and carried on getting into trouble there at QPR.

It was only a matter of time before I got my first banning order. The government had started to introduce powers to stop hooligans attending matches with exclusion orders.

I was at QPR v Derby with a load of my mates from Teddington; we were all over Derby and should have been 3 or 4 nil up. In the last ten minutes Dean Saunders popped up and scored an undeserved winner in my eyes.

I had the right hump, and in those days I took defeat very personally and wanted to vent my anger somehow. I said to the lads I was going round to the away end to smack a Derby fan. A couple of the lads came with me, and as we got to the away end a load of Derby fans were boarding their coach. They could see I was fuming and starting laughing and gesturing toward me. I steamed toward them and climbed aboard the coach without any fear. Meanwhile a copper had seen my actions and grabbed me back off the coach. I resisted and started to resist arrest, and then the officer pushed me almost to the deck, I shouted for him to fuck off. Of course I was nicked and taken to Shepherds Bush old bill shop. I was so worried about being remanded in custody that I gave a false name and address so as to get bail; it worked!

About two weeks after this I went to a Chinese Restaurant in Teddington with my mate from Hendon, also a QPR fan. I got into a bit of aggro there and ended up smashing the window. Again I ended up back on a blue mattress in a cell at Twickenham Police station. I had now lost count of the times I had been here.

As I woke up with a mouth like sandpaper and a head like a hammer drill; with that dreaded thought of trying to remember what had happened last night. Then it all came back to me, another criminal damage charge on the cards for sure.

The copper stood there smirking, "Do you want the good news or the bad news?" I was in no mood to be playing silly games right now, "Whatever" I replied sharply.

PC happiness informed me that I was a lucky boy and that the manager of the Chinese restaurant was not going to press any charges for the smashed window.

"Result!" I was thinking; and then the bombshell. "You are wanted by Shepherds Bush Police for breaching bail conditions and supplying false details. "You're in a bit of bother chap", now I really hated the contented look on this officer of the law's face.

I was to remain here for the day and be taken to

West London Magistrates Court in the morning.

It was the usual procedure of being picked up by a sweatbox and carted off to court. We arrived just before the hustle and bustle of the Monday morning rush hour through the streets of West London. The court was just down a road opposite the Olympia exhibition centre and not far from the main A4 in to Central London.

In these situations I always hoped I would get out back to freedom and down the pub by lunchtime!

A duty solicitor came to see me in a small room and asked of my account of the Derby incident. I told him, I was going to plead guilty, I could not be bothered with all the rigmarole of doing a not guilty, and it was not exactly a murder charge was it!

The brief then told me that the copper who nicked me stated that I had punched him to the side of the head when he restrained me off the coach.

"No way" I pleaded with the solicitor. He said he would see what he could do; if I pleaded guilty they may take that into consideration.

For some miraculous reason the CPS (prosecution) agreed if I went guilty they would not mention about any punch being thrown.

To cut a long story short I got a six week prison sentence for threatening behaviour and a two year exclusion order from all football matches in the UK.

What a double bummer I was to spend Christmas inside and not be able to go to my beloved Rangers for two years.

I was taken to Pentonville in North London. Six weeks did not seem a long sentence, but even just one day is long enough when you are behind the door in any prison. Luckily I was given a job, and that was to use a sewing machine, stitching chef's trousers. These trousers were for prison use and for hotels and restaurants on the outside.

To get to the workshop where I was working we had to walk through an old disused wing. On the top landing I could see a trap door, and I was told this was where prisoners were hung back in the day. It was very cold, silent and creepy in this wing, almost as if the tormented spirits of those hung inmates were still there.

On one of the first exercises I went out on the yard there was a stark reminder of prison life. On exercise we had to walk round in single file around a courtyard manned by screws at each corner.

Out of the blue a lad ran over to this big fella and looked as though he had slapped him across the face. But then the lad held his face as blood poured down his cheek onto the ground.

The inmate that did this was rushed by screws and bundled away sharply. The lad who had been cut was also led away quickly, exercise was cut short and we were all taken back to our cells.

The next day I saw the heavy set lad that had been cut on exercise again. I managed to ask him what that was all about. He told me that he had owed a debt for a quarter ounce of tobacco, not exactly a fortune. Currency inside was usually tobacco (burn) or spliff or even batteries. This showed me that there was no messing around in here; it was all about keeping pride or face.

The other act of aggro I saw in here was in the sluice room. In those days there were no toilets in cells, so a bucket was used. In the sluice room there was always trouble due to people spilling piss or something as petty.

One morning there was a big black lad who was a ringer for Evander Holyfield the boxer. Another black lad threw what looked like a jug of boiling water into his face. When I next saw him, the fella's face had turned pink in areas. I found out that the jug contained boiling water and sugar, which acted like Napalm and stripped the poor geezers' skin off. This was called "Jugging", something I hoped never happened to myself.

Christmas Day came and went and I was released the day before New Years Eve!

The first place I went to when I got out? Yes it was the Builders Arms; all the usual suspects were in there. I took a bit of stick for getting myself banged up again and would I ever learn.

I was still living in the room at the flat with Jason, he was hardly ever there anyway. I started knocking around with a mate who was younger than me; Alan. Alan was like Marmite, you either loved him or hated him, a lot of people didn't like him but I had a soft spot for him.

Alan was a proper thief, he liked burgling houses, I wasn't into this, and I always tried to keep a bit of moral pride about me. I had been involved in shop burglaries and other petty thieving and shoplifting but not private property.

The local lads all started going to the acid house parties and raves, they all seemed to be losing weight fast and getting all loved up. Although I liked the music, I was still into the football violence; my image was to be hard not to be a hippy type wearing psychodelic clothing and bandanas.

I had never taken an Ecstasy pill or never even wanted to, to be fair. Jason used to come back to the flat early in the morning some weekends and was off his nut. It did not appeal to me for some reason.

Saying this, myself and Alan started getting right on the speed, Alan also loved a spliff. Any time I smoked cannabis I would get really paranoid and did not enjoy it one bit. The speed was a different story, it allowed me to drink more and for longer.

I never once went in a house with Alan, I could not bring myself to do it, but I was happy to let Alan buy the booze and speed with the takings.

A new clothing store opened up in Teddington High Street and it sold all the latest clobber. Labels such as Duffer, Chipie, Timberland and the latest thing were Paisley patterned shirts. Dungarees were also in fashion right now, so the casual scene had turned into a hippy kind of trend.

We decided to rob the new shop; we went there in the middle of one night and got in through a back window. There were no alarms, how easy this was, too easy in fact. We had not planned this is any way, it was a spur of the moment thing, all we came armed with was a few black dustbin bags.

Alan filled up the bags with clothing and a few pairs of Timberland boots. We ran back to the flat across the sports field laughing hysterically all the way. When we got back up to the flat we emptied the contents on to my bed.

We would easily sell this the next day and keep a few bits for ourselves. We did get rid of the booty rapidly and went out to the pub in our new garments. I felt a million dollars, even though I had lost loads of weight due to the speed taking; I hardly ever ate any more.

Prior to this a few weeks back, I had been arrested in Richmond for Affray. A load of us had gone out and one of the lads had his pregnant girlfriend with him.

England was to play Wales in the Rugby next day and there were loads of Welsh supporters in Richmond this night. One of the Taffs decided to touch the pregnant girl and commented something like "How about going halves on another!"

I wasn't going to stand for this and smacked the fella straight on the nose; this triggered a western style brawl. Apparently I was hit side on by two of the Welsh fans from either side; I fell and knocked myself out on the brass rail that goes round the bar for your feet to rest.

When I came to, I smashed a half pint glass on the bar and chased out the retreating Welsh down the road. The old bill was already on the scene in no time and I was nicked, glass in hand. At the time I did not remember any of this and to this day it is only what I have been told.

The morning after in Richmond police station, when I awoke in the cell, I rang the bell to speak to an officer. The sergeant came to the hatch in the door; I asked him what I was doing here.

The sarge went away and came back with a small exhibit case with a broken glass inside it.

"Do you not remember this?"

I told him I remembered nothing, he informed me I had been threatening the Welsh lads with the said item.

I was charged with Affray and somehow got out on bail, I was well lucky.

That as I said was before the clothes shop burglary, as if I did not have enough on my plate!

Literally two days after we did the shop over, we decided to go back again, it was so easy.

We went back again in the middle of the night and found that alarms had still not been fitted. All that had been done was wire meshing had been put around the window frames.

We tried breaking the metal away, but had no joy, so Alan decided to go home and get some wire cutters. It took us no longer than half an hour to get back with the cutters.

In the meantime someone must have heard us trying to get in and had called the police. As we went round the back of the shop, there was a van full of coppers; they took one look at us and ran toward us both.

It is amazing how fast you can run when being chased by the law; I must have been not far off Linford Christie's 100 meter record.

I was caught this time, I did not see where Alan

went, but there was an Iceland shop right next door and Alan had jumped in a dumped chest freezer outside the store.

All the usual procedure followed, been taken to Twickenham police station, the removal of belongings, the bang up, lying on a blue mattress and the ultimate worry of what the charge was going to be. And even more the sheer hope of getting out on bail.

Even I doubted any chance of being set free this time, there was still the outstanding Affray case and now this.

After speaking with duty solicitors, we were both in the cells for the whole weekend and back up at Richmond on Monday.

The first time I saw Alan again was when we were taken up the stairs into the dock in court. Alan was limping and stank of fish, no word of a lie!

As we awaited for the magistrate to appear I asked Alan what had happened. He told me that when he jumped in the freezer to hide, he twisted his ankle; it looked nasty and was black and swollen.

Alan also did not realize that the freezer must have broken in the shop and still had fish in it. Anyway the coppers had found him in the freezer, what a sight and what a smell.

I felt for Alan, he was in agony, to top it off we had no smokes; I smoked back in those days.

The magistrate came in, our names read out and then the charges; Attempted Burglary, and Burglary. We had both gone no comment at the station but the police still presumed we committed the first burglary as we were there again.

What a pair of idiots we were, going back so soon to the scene of the crime; I suppose we deserved it for taking such a liberty. But at the time I always felt hard done by, I was more gutted I had lost my liberty and wasn't able to go to the pub, get pissed and see the lads.

The police had gone back to the flat and confiscated everything, and all the clothing I was wearing including the brand new Timberland boots were also bagged up and kept. I had Jason's expensive leather jacket as well, he would have been pissed off about that.

Bail was refused; it was not looking too good. We ended up going straight to Wormwood Scrubs.

While we were on remand, the old bill visited Alan

and he agreed if he was going to plead guilty they would waiver about 15 TIC's. The police knew Alan was committing burglaries in the area and had a load of unsolved cases. So he went along with the TIC's (taken into consideration).

There was not a day that I did not worry about how long I was going to get. At first we were going to deny the charges but after solicitors advice agreed to plead guilty.

For the Affray charge I was going to use mitigation that I was knocked out and did not remember a thing; which was actually true. But my brief pointed out that if I did not know what I was doing; I could have been capable of killing someone with the broken glass. I agreed to disagree but in the end thought better of it and went guilty.

It was a long stint on remand, I even ended up seeing the boxer Terry Marsh in both Scrubs and Brixton, and he was in for the alleged shooting of his promoter Frank Warren. What I liked about Terry was that he was one of your own, not up his own arse at all, he was a World Champion.

After six months finally we were to go up to Kingston Crown Court for sentencing. The day was at long last here. I crossed my fingers and every other body part and hoped for a twelve month sentence that would mean I would be out due to the time already served.

7 TRIP TO THE ISLE OF WIGHT

Alan only had one other previous conviction, which he received a two year prison sentence also for burglary.

Crown Court judges do not look very friendly; this one was a typical character, with white wig and half crown glasses. And yes he had the glasses at the end of his nose and looked down through them at us!

I was sentenced first; my heart was playing the bongo drums right now. Burglary 12 months imprisonment, Attempted Burglary 15 months, Affray 18 months. I tallied that up in my head quickly, that was a total of three years and nine months; holy shit!

Then came the word that saved the day, "to run

concurrently". The judge went on to say that the prison term for the Affray was so harsh because it seemed that every time there was a sporting event I looked to be involved in some kind of violence. That fight in Richmond had nothing to do with Rugby or sport at all, but I had no chance to defend my actions as I had pleaded guilty. The barrister explained to me afterwards that the judge had handed a longer term for the attempted burglary because it was an absolute act of cheekiness to have gone back the second time.

Alan was given another two year prison sentence, Judges hated burglaries and I believe he got a long sentence because of the house burglaries that had been TIC'd.

We ended up going to Wandsworth and then Pentonville for allocation. Allocation was a decision of what prison to see the sentence out at. I fell out with Alan a few times when we had shared a cell and also with a couple of other cell mates. What I did not know was that all these things are recorded by screws and there is a file kept on your behaviour.

When I was finally told where I was going, I was shocked and well gutted. I was going to Camp Hill on the Isle of Wight.

I asked why I was going to the Isle of Wight, and the reason I was given was because of my violence. I was not exactly a mass murderer, but I later worked it out that my outbursts with Alan and other cellmates had an impact on where I was going.

I was taken in a big green coach and we stopped off in Portsmouth at HMP Kingston, which was a prison just for lifers. We dropped off one inmate who even had a budgie in a cage with him. My little 18 month sentence was nothing compared to what this fella had to serve.

I was glad to be pulling away from that nick! On the coach we were seated two of us together facing two other prisoners and we were all handcuffed to chains going through our legs.

Someone commented to one of the screws aboard, what would happen if we started sinking; as we were now on the car ferry going across the Solent.

The officer joked that we were as good as Harry Houdini and could swim fast! Not really funny, but I suppose you had to laugh.

The Isle of Wight had three prisons all up the same road. As we entered the long road up a hill, so that was why it was called Camp Hill. There was Albany on the left; this was known as Paranoid City among the inmates. We delivered a few lads there, and then across the road to the right was the notorious Parkhurst. Only one inmate got out here, I didn't pity him at all, Parkhurst was a Category A prison for serious criminals, killers and terrorists.

So here I was at Camp Hill my home for next few months. It did not look too bad; the grounds were well kept with flower beds etc. It was not a typical Victorian prison with spurred wings.

I spent the first night with a loon named Les, funny how you remember some people's names and not others!

The cell we shared was ridiculous; there were two single beds with a toilet separating them. That was barbaric; we had to take a shit with a man right next to our heads. Oh well it was only for one night.

The wings at Camp Hill were named after Saints, strange how they come up with names for prison wings!

I ended up at James wing right at the top. Luckily this was not too bad, although they were all three man cells.

One of the fellas I was in with had been sentenced

to Four and a half years for killing a baby while drink driving. He told me he had driven home pissed one night and as he went over a humped bridge, he took off the road and went straight into a girl pushing her kid in a pram. The baby was killed instantly.

This bloke was in a real mess, both mentally and physically, he could not bear the guilt he felt. He showed me his wedding photos, to be fair he had been a good looking fella and in good shape. Now he had grey hair and was as thin as a beanpole. This should have served as stark warning for anyone considering drunken driving.

Before I was even remanded and back in the flat with Jason, my speed taking had taken its toll on me. I had become a paranoid wreck, and also was skinny and ill looking. Maybe this sentence had saved me, who knows. I went to the gym at every opportunity and from day one I had stopped smoking. For what I saw, smoking only got you in grief in prison, remember the lad who got cut in Pentonville?

Would you believe it, I saw that same lad here in Camp Hill; he had a neat little scar right down his face. Here he was serving another sentence and so was I.

One thing is for sure, I met some characters while in prison, some diamond fellas and some outright horrible fuckers. I only really want to remember the good ones.

I got my head down in Camp Hill and kept my nose clean so to speak. I was given the chance to go on Community Service, working outside the prison. Myself and a couple of others were to go and paint the inside of a community hall in Cowes. Part of the deal was that we were to stay in the premises and not go out anywhere. We were taken every morning in a van and picked up again later. This was all based on pure trust.

An older inmate, Eddie was with us, he was a typical East Londoner from Mile End. He was a veteran of doing time; he had previously served a long sentence for Armed Robbery. This time round he was doing a nine month sentence and he told me it was hurting him badly. Eddie was all settled down with a nice woman in his life, when he got into a bit of petty bother and here he was on the island. This short sentence was harder than the years he spent previously due to him missing the love of his life.

Eddie had come up with a grand plan, he was getting money sent to friends of a friend and they lived in Cowes themselves. He reckoned the house would only be about a ten minute walk from the hall.

There was a load of old donated clothing at the hall that we were going to put on so as to hide our prison uniform.

Part of the plan was to get the money and one of us would go in the supermarket across the road and get a load of cans of lager and have a bit of a jolly while we were painting away.

There was another lad with us, and his girlfriend was coming over for a visit. Eddie told him to ask his girl to come straight to the hall instead of going to the prison. This would have made a lot more intimate and personal for him.

A couple of days before I had got my hair cut back on the wing, and the geezer who did it swore he was able to do a decent job with the electric clippers. I wanted a short back and sides with different lengths blended in. To say he botched it up is an understatement! He messed it up so badly I decided I would have been better off shaving the lot off back to the bone with my disposable razor. I even managed to balls that up as I had loads of little shaving cuts to my head. When we went down that evening for tea, I had claret running down my face and neck from the nicks and I was bald as a coot.

I got some crazy looks from a lot of the fellas on the wing, they thought I was a new bod and looked like a psycho.

I was even pulled up by the senior officer that night who said he was close to putting me on a charge of changing my identity without permission.

So that was how I looked the day we were going to risk going out into the public to get the money to get pissed for the day.

We left the other lad to stay in the hall while we made our way down the road. We still had our blue prison trousers on with tatty old jumpers borrowed from the donations.

Eddie had a bit of paper with rough directions drawn on with the address written on. We were walking looking lost for a good twenty minutes; I started to get a bit edgy.

After a good half an hour we found the house we were looking for. I waited outside and Eddie went in and was back out in a couple of minutes.

"Bingo!" Eddie cheered as he came hurrying out with a small envelope in his hand. I never asked him how much cash he had, all I cared about was we were going to have a few beers. I had not had a drink for about eleven months now, and not due to choice.

By the time we got back to the hall we could see that there were coppers all over the place. There were two vans parked outside with a whole load of officers milling about inside.

"Shit we've been sussed" Eddie's understatement of the year!

Eddie darted back round the corner before he got seen and proceeded to shove the wrapped up cash up his backside. This was the best form of smuggling most items into a prison, and this tactic was often used on visits. It was know as "bottling".

It looked like our little party had been broken up and there was no sign of the other lad or his girlfriend.

We sheepishly turned back round the corner and headed back into the hall.

I was expecting to be pounced upon by the old bill, but in fairness they just asked where the hell we had been. We had already agreed to say as little as possible, so we just told them we had been for a walk.

When we got back to the prison we were not exactly welcomed with opened arms. We were taken straight to the block, which were the punishment cells for solitary confinement. We were to spend the night there and then the see the governor of the prison the next day.

One of the inmates who was a cleaner in the block came to our cell doors and quietly told us that we were famous.

The news on the local radio had announced that two prisoners had escaped and were headed toward the ferry in Cowes.

Because we had taken so long, we had been spotted by members of the public who had thought we were doing a runner from one of the prisons.

Eddie whispered through the cell hatch that we needed to come up with a feasible story to get us out of the shit.

It didn't take long to agree that I was going to say that I had started to get a severe headache from the paint fumes in the hall and Eddie offered to take me outside for a bit of fresh air.

The morning came and I was to see the governor after Eddie. I was led in by two screws that stood either side of me in front of the governor's desk.

I explained our alibi and was sure we would be dealt with leniently.

"I did not believe a word your partner in crime told me and I most certainly do not believe you either Casellas" the governor did not look happy and was going red in the face.

"I have never heard such a bullshit story and for your blatant attempt at lying to me and causing so much aggravation I sentence you to three weeks loss of remission"

Wow that hit me hard, that meant that my release date would be put back another three weeks; I only had five weeks to go so that was a real bummer.

Eddie had been moved to another wing and was apparently in a single cell on his own. I stayed where I was, and spent the next eight weeks sulking about our stupidity.

I heard through the grapevine that Eddie had lost the plot one day and smashed up his cell as he was so gutted at losing time, he was already struggling with this sentence.

I still made the most of it and kept going to the gym, I had never been as strong or fit in my life, and I was up to about 13 stones in weight.

I saw out my sentence with no more trouble and had spent a total of thirteen months inside.

8 ECSTASY

The day I was released was the greatest feeling I had ever felt, even more that QPR winning the second division in 1983.

I had planned with all my mates back in Teddington to have a reunion in the Lion pub that night.

The family that Mart lived with had kindly offered to let me move in again, they had moved to a different flat nearer Broad Street, which ironically was right opposite the electrical shop I had done time for before.

I had come out with all the good intentions of staying fit and keeping up the weight training which I did for about six weeks. Before I went to prison I could not see the attraction to Acid House parties and taking E's. I would never have considered it even though I was on the speed and still drinking like a fish almost every night.

My drinking never changed, that was my priority even with my new found fitness regime.

My good pal Mikey came round every Friday after my release and we went out as we always used to, to the local pubs.

Then one night he asked me would I want to do an E with him. To be honest I was slightly scared of what it would do to me. I had never been afraid of running into a load of geezers at football, so why not give it a go.

I remember that night and that feeling now as I write this. We started off in the Horse and Groom; there was always a good crowd in there those days. The duke box was playing all the latest dance tunes and everyone was in high spirits.

I took that first pill, it was a white Dove only a tiny little thing but it cost 15 quid, was it worth it?

Mikey said to just relax and go with the flow, and what happened next blew my mind. I was sitting down in the seats around the wall of the pub generally chatting and listening to the tunes.

Then all of a sudden I had this warm intense feeling

come right up through my body. And as it hit my face my mouth opened and I stood up like an Emperor in Rome. My arms were held aloft and I started shouting out; "Fuckin Hell, Fuckin Hell!" and then I started joining in with the song on the duke box. What a fitting tune it was; "All together now" by the Farm. I had just come out of nick and here we were all together in the pub and I was rushing on my first ever E.

My gosh!, now I could see what the fuss was all about, that night was a golden nugget of an experience.

Myself and Mikey went to Richmond and ended up in a small basement nightclub up at the top of the bridge. We pulled a couple of girls that night and ended up taking them back to Mikey's. Mikey still lived with his mum and stepdad whom I had lived with several years ago.

We were so off our heads it really did not matter where we were. We both got our ends away and it was a perfect end to my first dabble with Ecstasy.

The funny thing was the next morning, after we had managed to get a bit of sleep, the girls had gone. That was ok as they had a left a phone number, they said they were from Blackburn or somewhere up North.

When we tried to call them the phone went to a dead tone, they had given us a moody false number!

I was pretty much hooked straight away and couldn't wait for our next night out. Mikey had been going to a club called "The Park" in Kensington, and that is where we went for a while every Friday night.

This was the end of 1991 and the house scene was at a peak and the pills were very strong. I only ever really took Doves or Dennis the Menace's which were red and black capsules. Whenever I got on one, I would just dance like a madman for hours and just get right into the music. I could never really hold a conversation as I was so off my face. I continued to drink loads of pints, maybe not as much as I usually would.

A lot of ravers would call drinkers "beer monsters", I couldn't care less I loved my beer.

It is a fact that the rave scene and ecstasy impacted on a reduction in football violence as everyone was loved up. I didn't go to football as much and these E's had certainly calmed me down. I no longer went out just looking for trouble, the music had taken me over and it would be at least a Wednesday before I started to come down from the effects and buzz from the pills.

It was like being in a different world, that's why they call it Ecstasy, it sure did make you horny and there were times when girls just came up and starting snogging me out of the blue. This was Utopia and normal working life seemed like shit, I was now just living for my next E. I could hear the tunes in my head all week even at work on or on the train. I used to look at other people and examine the expressions on their face and almost convinced that everyone had been raving!

Another brilliant night was at Linford Studios at Battersea, I started raving in the queue outside. I could feel the bass beating through the walls and I had to stop myself dancing out on the pavement. It was almost impossible to stay straight faced when being searched by security; I always took my first E on the way, so I would be coming up while waiting to get in. Probably a bit of a waste of a buzz, but fuck it didn't matter where you where when you were like this!

The Friday night at Linford Studio was called The Temple, and it sure was a Temple for us worshippers of the rave scene. I saw Rat Pack there nearly every week and guest artists such as Crystal Waters who sang Gypsy Woman. The laser lights at Temple were amazing, and the rushes in there were immense.

I carried on working as a painter and a lot of the other painters were right into the dance scene as well. I've still got tapes mixed by some of the lads.

Another mate of mine Graham started hanging round with us and he became my weekend drinking and pilling partner.

One Saturday we decided to go up the West End and go to a club called Third Base in Shaftsbury's night club. As usual it was banging, and we were flying on Dennis the Menaces. I ended up getting involved snogging a girl and we hardly left each other's side that night. It was proper drug induced lust and I got her phone number.

I called Jan a few times before we agreed to meet up again in the West end. Jan was a waitress and lived in a flat in Kennington, right by the War Museum. Jan shared the flat with two Gay fellas, they were decent and a good laugh. The rave scene bought everyone together, and women felt safe clubbing with the Gay community as they had no agenda toward women and also loved a great time and dancing.

It wasn't long before I moved in with Jan and her friends, it was only a one bed flat and Jan used the front room as her bedroom. I was only there for about a month before the boys decided to move out and get their own place.

At the time we were paying £80 a week for the flat, this was 1992 and that seemed quite a lot at the time.

I liked living up at this end of London, we were right by Lambeth Walk and a stones throw from Waterloo station. There were some good pubs and cafes round here, and only a short bus ride into the West End over Westminster or Lambeth Bridge.

I managed to get a lot of work painting for various firms up here and I ended up working for a Maltese crowd who had a lot of contracts all around South London.

While I was working for this firm I met a body builder, Dave from Angel Town in Brixton. I started training hard again and we used to go to this shady gym in Camberwell. It was full of Yardies and other wannabe gangsters. They spent more time looking in the mirror or on their mobiles organizing drug deals than actually pumping any iron.

I started to get a good shape myself, but my only downfall was that my post workout drink was a few cans of Stella, while Dave's was a protein drink.

I started to knuckle down a bit while I was with Jan, and our nights out raving started to slow down.

There was one night when I had gone out on my own after work one Friday. I used to get paid cash in those days and many a time I would go for a couple with a few of the Maltese lads at work and just end up carrying it on, on my own.

This particular night, we had finished a job so I still had my tool bag with me and was still wearing dirty old T-shirt and jeans. I even had my white overalls in the bag with me. I left the others and decided to go into Elephant and Castle; I would sometimes get talking to others and there were times when I sat at the bar like Billy no mates.

I was bladdered and was probably staggering around, although I never saw that at the time. I had this mad idea to go to the Ministry of Sound on my own. The Ministry was a bit upper class a bit out of my league, but that didn't bother me at all; I just wanted to get right on one. I was sure I could score a pill or two while I was in the club.

There was a massive long queue waiting to get in, and I joined in. I did not speak to anyone while I waited; I was out of the game as I had so much to drink already. No one said anything to me either, the truth is they gave me a wide berth and must of thought I was some sort of nutter wearing filthy clobber and carrying a tool bag. It was either that or some crazy attempt at fancy dress; I had come as Dave the painter!

At last after what seemed like an hour or two, I got to the front of the queue. The bouncer took one look at me and said in disbelief; "Are you having a laugh?"

I didn't see the funny side and started to lose it and I offered him and his colleagues to fight there in the street.

Someone behind me warned me that I would be slaughtered, I did not give a shit and continued to scream at them, bag in hand.

Some how I got away with that one, by rights I should have taken a spanking for showing them up in front of the waiting crowd like that.

In the end I saw better of it and left, I was more gutted that I had waited all that time and not been allowed in. The madness was I just did not see the reasoning for being refused entry.

I was still knocking about with Graham and fair play he would often come up to see me and we would go out round the West End.

Graham was a wild card as well; I never knew what he was going to do next. It was Christmas time and we decided to do a pub crawl around Piccadilly and the Soho area. Graham had his new girlfriend with him; she was a local girl from Twickenham area and was a stunner. God knows how Graham used to pull girls like that but fair play to him, he was a laugh and sure had the bunny rabbit, and he could talk the hind legs off a donkey.

It was freezing cold and the crowds around Leicester Square and Shaftsbury Avenue were heaving along the pavements. The traffic as always was crawling along and every other vehicle was either a London Taxi or a red double decker bus.

There were groups out on their Christmas parties, and everyone was in the festive mood. We were enjoying ourselves and starting to get very merry indeed. Up ahead Graham spotted a tall fella and his helper another good looking young woman, it was obvious by their accents that they were South East Londoners. I can always tell what part of London someone comes from by their dialect. They were selling Santa hats, the ones with a bell on the end, how Christmasy.

Graham reached out and snatched one of the hats out of the fellas hand; he was a big chap and looked like he could handle himself if it came to it. Well it certainly was coming to it as Graham had just robbed the bloke for a poxy hat of all things.

In an instant it erupted and the fella who was wearing a Santa hat himself landed a good right hander on Graham's forehead. That must have hurt the guys hand, I was straight in throwing my own punches and then I felt a couple of blows to the back of head.

Santa's helper had taken off her shoe and was whacking me with it, by this time Graham was away down the road, leaving me to take another good hit straight under my eye. All the shoppers and office workers looked on in shock, Happy Christmas everyone!

I managed to break away and catch up with Graham and his girl further up the road. I now had blood pouring down my face from a cut under my eye. We went in a pub and I managed to get some tissue to clean up a bit.

Well that put a dampener on the proceedings; I stayed out for a few more and then parted company and went home to Jan.

Jan took one look at me and my eye had started to swell and bruise up. She shook her head, and commented that nearly every time I went out with Graham there was trouble. I tried to defend him out of loyalty for a mate, but truthfully Jan was right.

It got worse, just as I had convinced Jan I would keep out of trouble I went out with Graham during the Euro 92 football tournament. The night that England played Sweden we went out to Kingston to watch the match in one of the big sports bars along the river Thames.

True to form, I got hammered well before the match had started. I was pissed up that during the game I did not even realise that it was now the second half and England had changed ends. I could hardly stand let alone see the screen, Sweden scored and I let out a big roar thinking it was us who had hit the back of the net. Literally the whole bar which was crammed turned and stared at me.

Somehow I managed to explain my mistake to everyone. England was eliminated that night, so everyone was well pissed off.

We decided to walk back to Teddington which was a fair old trot along the river and over Teddington Lock Bridge. It must have taken three times as long as we both staggered along.

We went toward our destination, Graham's mate's house; we were going to crash there for the night. Graham nipped in to the side of a house and said he was going for a piss. I waited there by the gate for what seemed like ten minutes. I went round the back and there was no sign of him, after another minute or so he came running out with something in his hands.

Graham had only broke in to the big semi detached home, it was one of those properties that looked like well off people lived there.

Graham was grinning like a Cheshire cat. He said he had a load of cash, a blank cheque which had been signed and a bank card. There was even a bit of paper with what appeared to be a PIN number written on it. The owners must have been away and left the cheque for a cleaner or someone and the bank card with the PIN was maybe to pay some bills.

Graham headed straight to the nearest cash point about a five minute walk away which was on Teddington Bridge. It was now around 2am and we were the only people out and there were no cars on the roads.

We stood there in the dimly lit street at the opening in the wall, and Graham started cursing.

"Would you fucking believe it, I've lost the bit of paper with the PIN on it!" Graham shook his head furiously.

I do not know the exact odds on guessing a four digit number, must me multi millions to one. We were that stupid, we thought we would have a chance of cracking the code.

Just our luck a cop car went past, probably just patrolling around at that time of the morning. They looked straight at us but carried on going. Graham was adamant to keep tapping away at the keys until we got a result. Obviously we didn't; and then after a couple of minutes the police returned back up the road toward us.

"Fuck it, walk away is if nothing has happened, keep your head down and act calm" Graham ordered.

Graham proceeded to empty his pockets and throw the contents over a wall. I threw the cash he had given me away too.

The boys in blue pulled up right beside us and shouted at us to stand still and not move.

Basically the theme of the conversation was what we was doing at a cash point at 2am for over five minutes. It did all seem a bit strange, we should have walked away as soon as they had passed us the first time.

Both of us were searched, Graham was clear but out of my back pocket appeared the signed blank cheque.

I was not quick enough to think of a convincing reason to have this in my possession. So yet again I was cuffed and nicked. And off I went back to my old hotel that was Twickenham Police station.

Even though I was well steamed up on the beers and Jack Daniels, I did not sleep a wink in the cell that night.

I was questioned in the morning and gave no comment. I was told that a neighbour had seen Graham enter the property and they had called the police. We were both in the vicinity standing at a cash point like Dumb and Dumber, two and two makes four. Or in our case it made zero!

Cut another long story short, I was charged with Burglary. As I said before, I hated house burglary but was always happy to take any offerings.

I was kept in all weekend again; Jan made her way over from Kennington and visited me in the station. She bought some cigarettes and some chocolate. Jan also handed me a jelly rat bought from the newsagents.

"That's you," Jan was half fuming and half crying when she exclaimed what a rat I was. I was well choked, I really did not want to be in this situation again and certainly had not gone out that night with any intentions of getting in bother.

I remembered back to my time in Camp Hill and poor old Eddie who had been so gutted about being away from the love of his life.

Jan insisted that I should not take the rap for Graham; but me being loyal and not wanting to be a grass was going to have to take this one on the chin.

I had given a no comment statement, which did not show guilt or otherwise but it would also go against me in court.

Jan said I would have to ask Graham to give himself in and admit to the burglary. I never in a million years thought he would do that.

I was in the cell all weekend as usual and on the Monday morning a miracle occurred.

Graham produced himself at court and admitted to doing the house over; I could not believe it. That was what you would call getting someone out of Jail!

Due to all my previous I would have got at least two years; Graham had only one other petty conviction. Maybe the courts would be more lenient with him.

So as it now stood, Graham was charged with Burglary and I was slapped with a Handling Stolen Goods number. Surely I would walk for this. Anyway we were both remanded in custody.

For some reason all the prisons were full to capacity at the time so we had to spend time in Police custody. We both went to Bow Road cop shop in the East End. The weather was hot and the rest of the Euro 92 tournament was on.

We managed to get a radio bought in on a visit, so

we listened to the football. Against the odds, Denmark won the trophy, to be fair they had some good players around that time.

The good thing about police custody is that we were given the choice to ask for any food we wanted from the outside. We were in the cells for five weeks and there is only so much takeaway food you can eat.

Our case was to appear before a judge at Isleworth Crown Court in West London nearer my old manor of Teddington and Feltham.

We had both pleaded guilty and now it was a case of eagerly waiting for our sentence.

Graham received 12 months imprisonment and I was given six months. Six months for a blank cheque, my name was not Ronnie Biggs that's for sure.

We went to the Scrubs for about a week and because that was so full we were sent to HMP Oxford. Oxford had been closed down for years, but due to the lack of prison space it was reopened to take the slack.

I vowed to myself, this would be the last time I spent in prison, enough was enough.

9 CATFORD

It was very emotional being released and seeing Jan again, we still lived in Kennington in the flat.
I was able to get work painting again with the Maltese firm, and this was the ending of the recent recession where wages had gone right down.

Jan was now working in Ladbrokes the bookies as a cashier, so between us we were doing OK. Jan's brother had a good mate who was a Financial Advisor; so we asked him about mortgages.

I had been working with a bloke called Jim, he was a nutter just like me, but he was now settled down with a wife and grown up daughter. We had a great laugh on the sites we were on, even though Jim was from South East London he was a Chelsea fan. We used to have a lot of banter between us about that.

Jim lived in Catford, the other side of Lewisham; he

told me that properties were cheaper over this side of London. Myself and Jan did our research and Jim was right, apart from the poorest areas of east London this was probably as affordable as you could get anywhere in London at the time.

We viewed a couple of flats, and it did not take us long before we made an offer on a two bed flat with a back garden in Catford.

Our bid was accepted and we got a mortgage for £47.000. That was a great result as house prices were still recovering from the recession.

We had new UPVC windows fitted and I redecorated the whole flat. I asked a tiler on one of the sites I was working on to completely tile our bathroom. The flat was looking good, and we had four cats, one was a stray that came into our garden and we adopted him.

Was I finally taking responsibility and becoming an adult!? I had a good long run of staying trouble free, although I still drank every night after work, even if it was only four cans of Stella; ONLY!

Jan loved a bottle or two of red wine each evening and a spliff or two. I did not smoke as it just made me go into myself and start getting depressive and anxious thoughts, so it was not for me.

We had both not taken E's for a while now and life was stable. Every now and then I would go and see the lads over in Teddington, usually if there was a party or a do. A couple of my mates DJ'd and they often put on their own nights.

Now I was over this side of London I drank with the lads from work and I would still do my vanishing act of staying out on my own. I would go drinking in some very dodgy pubs in Lewisham, Deptford and Woolwich.

When I was in Lewisham I would end up drinking with Millwall supporters or travellers, I certainly did not weigh up any risks or danger. I always got away with my bare faced cheek. I would start singing QPR songs on my own, and there was a couple of times I got a bit of a kicking outside pubs at closing time.

I have to admit that I was unfaithful to Jan; I often ended up sleeping with other women that I managed to pull in pubs. One of my conquests was a well spoken girl, she lived up in Crystal Palace, I had been out with a mate from work and I remember that there was a live Boxing match on TV involving Gary Stretch.

I was so full of myself that I convinced this lady that I had been Gary Stretch's sparring partner and I was training for my first professional fight. I had never done any boxing in my life, only the scraps at football and pubs over the years.

When I had my nose smashed that time, the operation had left me with a very flat hooter. I was always being asked if I was a boxer.

After a lot more drinking and more bullshitting I went back to her house. So many times I had awoken in places and not remembered how I got there let alone who I was with.

I certainly did not remember the name of this woman, she was very attractive and this appeared to be a very well kept property with expensive furnishings.

I tried it on again, but she explained to me that she felt guilty as her husband was away working abroad. That was a proverbial blow right between my legs. It put me off straight away and I got out of there fast, although for some reason I asked for her number but she refused.

When I got back to Jan that morning, she smelled a rat immediately. She began questioning me about who had I been with. All the times I had stayed out before Jan had never asked this from me.

I did feel a bit guilty and my face was never going to live up to a lie; so I admitted what had happened. Jan said she knew as she could smell another female on me. Jan was a cat lover, so just like a feline she must have had extra sensory smell.

Jan did not go mental, although she did cry and we did not split up over my act of adultery. This was not the first time and would not be the last. In fact I found out later that Jan had a little fling with her manager at the bookies. And to be honest I could not really blame her.

We carried on with our lives; I continued to work, drink and still went to football every now and then. Myself and Jan did go out together to the cinema or a restaurant, life was not too bad.

I had a good relationship with Jan's brother, he was a big Spurs fan, and so was she. I went to the odd game with them, I did like White Hart Lane, and it was an impressive stadium.

We went to Spurs v QPR one season; we did well and won 3-1. I was up in the main stand with them both and went crazy every time we scored. It was only because I was with Jan and her bro that I probably got away with getting a good hiding!

I did this again at another match, QPR played Charlton away in the League Cup. I managed to get two tickets from a good old fella that I was working with. He had a season ticket and was going away for a couple of weeks and let me use his season ticket and another complimentary for the main stand at Charlton.

I promised my colleague I would behave myself, but me being me, I could not help myself. When our keeper Tony Roberts saved a penalty I cheered like we had won the match; which we lost 1-0. Again I got away with murder somehow, Jan was not impressed.

Another very embarrassing incident for Jan was when I went out on one of her firm's parties in a pub in Brixton. It was a leaving do for one of her colleagues; they had worked there for years. There was going to be a few big wigs there, and Jan pleaded with me to behave.

I can't remember the name of the pub, but it was down a back street right by a dodgy estate. The pub was full a good old Irish establishment with a mix of older generation builders and a load of younger lads. The evening started well, I was making good conversation and being polite and friendly with her area supervisor. If I remember rightly he was a York City fan so we had a good chat about football.

The bar we were in started to get really packed and a little group of young chaps walked in. One of them bumped into me and I spilled a bit of my pint down myself.

"Sorry about that son!" the tallest lad exclaimed loudly.

I was convinced that the geezer was mocking me, so I replied "Who the fuck are you calling son?"

Jan saw all of this going on and could not believe what I had just said. Everything after that happened very rapidly. The landlord, a very thick set Irishman had shot round from behind the bar and grabbed me in a bear hug from behind.

I could not move, and hen the lad who I had exchanged words with began punching me. He landed a beauty under my eye and a few other digs in to my ribs. A few other boys also started to get involved, all the time I was screaming at them to "have it" and was offering them all out. Jan's manager who was from Belfast managed to grab me from the landlord and begin bundling me out of the pub. All the time I was still going mental and wanting to fight my attackers. Lenny, Jan's boss must have calmed the situation and he told me to just go home, I was still standing in the middle of the road beckoning the group with my hands.

Jan finally shut me up and we got down the road to a cab office.

The next morning I had a lovely black eye and a good lecture from Jan. I could not apologize enough, but the damage had been done and yet again I had broken a promise.

Jan must have been contemplating how she could ever calm me down because she suggested that we try and have a child. I half heartedly agreed, maybe it was time to bring an offspring into this world.

Jan had a cyst on her ovary which meant that pregnancy would be a hard task. We were able to be granted IVF treatment on the NHS. Jan started the treatment at St Thomas's hospital, Westminster. I even went along to learn how to administer injections for the treatment.

After a month or so Jan started to get nasty side effects and felt quite ill. We agreed that Jan would stop the IVF and we would have to just take our chances.

Not long after this, Jan suggested we get married, at first I was totally against the idea. In the end I agreed to get wed, I did love Jan in my own mad way.

We got married on the isle of Gibraltar, my dad had now moved to Spain and he had lost his second wife Lynn a year or so prior to this.

Dad had met another lady who had also lost her husband so they hit it off straight away.

We asked Dad if we could get married in Alicante where he lived, but that was out of the question as we needed to be residents of Spain. However Gibraltar was still governed by the UK so we could have our wedding there. Dad drove us down and we stayed in a hostel in a really old traditional Spanish town not far from Gibraltar.

Jan kicked off about the lack of privacy in our room, which to be fair she was right. That night over dinner I erupted and told dad that I wanted to kill him. I did not know where that outburst had come from, but it was out and there was no turning back.

My good old mate Tony from Feltham agreed to be

my best man, he was already on holiday in Southern Spain so he had come down with his other half Lucy to stay in a hotel on Gibraltar. Myself and Jan were lucky enough to get a room there too, and we left Dad and Viv at the old hostel.

Fair play to Dad he turned up at the registry office, the same one that John Lennon had married Yoko Ono at. It was a very personal and intimate wedding; we even managed to drag someone off the streets to be our witness when we signed the register!

Fair play to Dad, he paid for a massive table in a classy restaurant with waiter service and we got through a series of dishes and loads of booze. The weather that day was blinding sun and after the meal, we all went down to the harbour and sat at the waterfront in a bar drinking more.

Dad and Viv made their excuses and went back to the hostel in mainland Spain and we all went back to the hotel bar. Funnily enough there was an American couple who had just wed at the same registry office that day and we all got hammered on Tequila slammers and anything else we could slurp down.

To say we all had a hangover from hell the next

morning would be an understatement.

I was now a married man, although it made no difference to me. The way I saw it was we had been living together from the off so to be married was just a piece of paper in my opinion.

I was well settled in sustaining work and earning decent wedge, Jan was pulling in a regular wage too. We had opened a joint bank account before we got the mortgage and to be honest I did splash out too much on the piss and my days at football.

I had gone a long run of staying out of the courts, and after the Brixton pub palaver I had tried to make a bit of effort.

Another old pal of mine who was Mart's half brother had started a successful business; he was doing a bit of property maintenance for his step dad. The work was for one of the biggest property companies in the UK; we are talking about shopping centres and massive warehouses and the like.

Simon got me some decent painting jobs, and I was still working with Jim from Catford. One of the jobs was to paint the corridors and landings at an office block in Ilford, Essex. We had a great laugh there; we had to paint the doors to the offices. While I was applying my magic to one of the doors there was a young secretary sitting at her desk. It was like a fantasy, she had long blondish hair tied up and she wore those sexy secretarial glasses. We kept looking at each other and just smiling, the sort of smile that said "I want to get you in bed!"

It didn't take me long before I had chatted this lovely into going out for a night. We had already planned to work the weekend and that was my alibi to tell Jan, I was going to stay in a B and B in Ilford and crack on and earn a good bit of money.

Myself and my sexy secretary went straight to the pub; as usual I was steaming and couldn't wait to get my conquest back to our room. It was great we jumped straight on each other and it was pure drunken lust. She was a kick-boxer so had a bit of a girly six pack, which turned me right on.

The next morning we had a shower and drove to the job, as we got out of the car her hair was still wet. Simon's business partner John was outside the entrance and shook his head in disbelief when he saw the pair of us.

Simon later told me that John wasn't happy about what I had been up to. John took things a bit seriously, he was trying to make a name for himself and make the business very successful. The doors we had painted in the corridors looked decent; but one morning when we came in me and Jim saw John lying on the floor checking the bottoms of the doors. John had noticed a tiny little miss about a couple of millimetres and had made us go round the doors again and re-coat them.

Still we did not let that bother us as we had earned some good dosh on this job, and I had the added bonus of getting my end away.

Simon at this time was living in a kind of half way house in Hounslow; there were a couple of girls living there and another fella Les. I ended up staying there a few nights, and Simon had also pulled a girl at the job that went on to say he had got her pregnant. But that is another story for Simon to tell.

One weekend we arranged to take the girls up the West End, it was the same day as the last game of the season in 1995-96. Qpr were playing West Ham at home and we needed to win or we were going to be relegated out of the Premier League. I could not believe myself that I was missing this game, but the lure of my new fling outweighed the football this time.

We ended up in a few pubs around The Strand and

Shaftsbury Avenue; it didn't take too long for me to get steaming as I knocked them back at a rapid pace. I was desperate to find out how my team had got on; so we went in a bookies right by Trafalgar Square.

I walked in and ask the punters in there, did they know the Qpr score. An old Irishman called over that we beat West Ham 3-0. I let out a massive roar and started to do a little jig, much to the amusement of the girls.

"Don't celebrate too fast mate!" another bloke in the bookies chirped back at me. "Qpr have still been relegated!"

I was mortified, and stormed out the shop and marched up the street like the Terminator. I found out later that other results had not gone our way and even though we won, we still were relegated.

I acted like a proper dick-head and threw a big wobbly; Simon screamed at me that he was showing us up in front of the girls. They did not seem too phased by my behaviour and we ended up going back to Hounslow to an Indian restaurant.

I loved a good curry, especially when I had had a good skin full of booze. We got ourselves a nice table for four right in the corner by the window and ordered loads of starters. One of my favourites was all the sauces and chutneys and I spooned these on to popadoms and naan breads.

Again Simon said I was making a pig of myself and it was embarrassing. The girls did not agree and stated that at least I was enjoying myself. Simon got stressed too easily and acted like an old woman sometimes.

At least my behaviour had been good in the curry house; back in the day a load of us would go after closing time at the pub and use the restaurant as an excuse to keep drinking. We would abuse the Indian waiters and make their lives a misery.

There was one time that about ten of us went to the Indian in Hampton Wick, one of our mates was on leave from the army and had a mate with him. We ordered loads of food and plenty of pints; the bill came to about £250 that was a lot in the mid 1980's.

We all steamed behind the counter and through the kitchen past the chefs and waiters. They looked on in amazement as we had to literally jump a ten foot wall to get away. Somehow we did mange to escape; there was a story in the local paper that week with the headline; "Gang go for a curry in a hurry!"

Anyway, this evening with the girls went well and myself and Simon paid the bill, we had a good feed and headed back to Simon's room at the house. The house was a massive four story Victorian building, and there was an attic room which was currently vacant.

I led my girl up to the top, and she insisted we were not having any sex. I was pissed off to say the least. I asked her if it had been due to my behaviour today. She gave me an ultimatum that I had to leave my wife and show that I was serious about her. I had already been too honest and explained I was married. I told her I was not prepared to leave Jan so that was the end of that. Life just ticked along, I grafted to earn money to keep paying the mortgage and bills with Jan, which was an equal venture.

The house was in good order, we still had the cats and Jan had her mates and I had mine. To be honest we were sort of living separate lives, we still went out together but it was not a very close marriage like a lot of couples you would see.

It was 1999; three years later; myself and Jan had

just come back from a holiday in Faliraki on the Greek Island of Rhodes. I had behaved like a twat to Jan and probably ruined her holiday. I had treated it like a lad's holiday and not a nice break away with my wife. I just got hammered from morning to night and even shouted at her in front of everyone in the hotel because I wanted to go out on my own one night. I had never been on a lad's holiday when I was younger due to all the trouble I got myself into; i.e. paying fines or spending time in nick. Poor Jan had to put up with me running riot and treating the holiday like I was a single bloke.

We had only been back a week from Rhodes and Qpr were playing Fulham at Craven Cottage. This was the first time we had played our neighbours in many years and everyone was well fired up for it.

The tickets for us were selling out fast; we had the whole Putney end and a section of seats in the riverside stand. What was apparent on the day itself was that Qpr had got tickets in almost every part of the ground.

I decided to go even though I had no ticket, but was going to get a ticket off a mate in the pub when I got there. Loads of us met up in the Golden Gloves in Fulham Palace Road, there were faces there from the past and every man and his dog had turned out for this one. Everyone was buzzing, and the weather was still pretty decent. I felt great; I still had a good tan from holiday and was wearing a new short sleeve Lacoste checked shirt.

The only tickets that any of the lads had left were for the Stevenage Road terrace which was for home fans only. At least that section of the ground was right by the away terrace.

As usual the old bill had been keeping an eye on everyone and in this day and age they were filming who they thought were possible trouble-makers on hidden cameras and sometimes blatantly with camcorders in their parked vans.

I had a ticket and was well pleased; at least I could soak in the atmosphere and watch us play our nearest neighbours. Surely we had to win this one; Fulham had been making their way back up the divisions after a bad spell for years. And we had only been down from the Premier league for a couple of years.

As we all walked to the ground I had that excited feeling in my stomach like butterflies; I had not felt like this for any match for a long time. Qpr fans were everywhere and were piling into the away end. I saw a little queue of our lads getting into the

Stevenage Road turnstile. There seemed to be a lot of us going in there. The word was that Fulham should have given us more tickets and that would have solved any segregation issues.

About ten of us made our way through the crowd and stood at the back of terrace, there were seats up behind us with a small drop from the seats to the standing area. I was so pissed by now, and could not really take it all in. I could tell that the Fulham fans knew we were Qpr and already there was tension in the air.

Just before the players had come out of the tunnel one of our lot started up a Qpr song, and before we had even finished our chant, punches had been thrown and all hell broke loose. It all happened so quickly, all I remember was I was now down the front with my back up against the hoardings by the pitch side. Fulham fans were rushing in from all over and I stood facing them fending them off. Before I knew it I was being ripped out of the terrace and onto the pitch. I thought I had been nicked and to my disbelief, whoever had grabbed me had let me go. There were now loads of Qpr fans being led and making their way to the packed away terrace.

As I was about to step into the Qpr end, a copper

grabbed me then; he marched me through the players tunnel which led to an exit onto the street. I was let go there and told to fuck off home.

What a result, I was free to go, but then again I had not really done anything to warrant being arrested anyway in my eyes. As soon as I came out the ground there were still Qpr fans trying to get in and a well known lad Mark G came straight over to me and pointed out that my shirt buttons had been ripped off. My shirt was hanging open, and I was also minus my new baseball cap. That was a bummer; I tried to tuck the shirt in to make myself look a bit more respectable.

A lad called Paul from Brixton was with Mark and we ended up standing around chatting for a while. We were told to move on and get away from the ground. We found a pub a little further up one of the side streets there and had a pint. Paul suggested we try and go back to the ground and see if we could get back in the Qpr end somehow. By now it was half time, and as we walked past the big Hammersmith end for home fans we spotted a couple of our lads in there.

One of the boys came running down when he saw us; I went over to the big iron gates at the entrance and told him all about what had happened earlier. I also asked him the score and did he know any other half time scores as I had a bet on a few matches.

We walked up to the away end but it was all locked up now, we had no chance of getting in, I decided to part company with Mark and Paul and go for a walk back up toward Fulham Palace Road.

I hung around until near the end of the match and went back to the ground; I wanted to wait for all my pals to come out and carry on the evening with them.

We lost 1-0, and there were a lot of very pissed off Qpr fans storming out the ground. There was a massive police presence trying to separate us and Fulham coming out the Stevenage Road end, they were obviously unhappy that Qpr had been in all their ends and had it not been for the old bill it would have been mayhem on the streets. A few lads were being nicked as they were getting over excited. It took police what seemed like ages to clear all the crowds. I saw some of my mates again and we made our way back toward Hammersmith. The whole of the Fulham Palace Road was a sea of Qpr fans. And even though we had lost the game, most of the talk was about all the trouble in and around the ground.

Some of the Sunday papers had reported about the trouble and it had even been on the radio that day about it being like the 1980's all over again.

Jan was worried that I had nearly been arrested again, and to be honest so was I. On the Monday there was a write up in the London Evening Standard that Met Police were studying CCTV footage of the day and were confident of making arrests. I had been so drunk on the day it had all been over in a blink, almost like I had been in a black-out. I was sure I had nothing to worry about otherwise I would have been nicked there and then; wouldn't I?

I was painting around the Streatham and Norbury area at the time and one lunchtime a mate of mine Neil rang me on my mobile. This was about three weeks after the Fulham game; I had not been back to Qpr since, as I wanted to keep a low profile. Neil told me that the FIU (football intelligence) had been looking for me. They knew who I hung around with and had approached Neil and suggested to him that I contact them if I did not want my door kicked in one morning. They had even given Neil a number for me to call them on at Fulham police station. As it happened the office for the FIU for West London was based down Fulham Road.

I rang them and made an appointment for me to go and see them. I honestly thought I would be in and out and even arranged for Jan to come with me so we could go for a meal afterwards.

I was expecting to be interviewed by Conway who was the main copper in charge of the Qpr FIU. Instead there was a detective sergeant, not associated with football that was in charge of this case. I had not bothered bringing a solicitor with me, as I thought I would not need one. The DS asked me did I want to call a brief; I just wanted to get away and go for a meal so I declined.

I was led into an interview room with the DS and another FIU copper who I already knew from the matches at Qpr home and away. I broke the golden rule and gave a statement, I should have just gone "no comment" to every question; but as I said I thought this was a formality with no charge.

I was shown photos of me standing outside the Golden Gloves pub with some of my mates, which proved nothing. Then I was shown a still from the CCTV footage of me in the Stevenage Road terrace. It showed me down by the pitch surrounded by three stewards raising my arm up toward oncoming Fulham fans.

I explained everything had happened in a split second, which it had and I was just defending myself from being attacked which also was true.

The problem was that I was well pissed, and when I got pissed I could lose it a bit. I was not shown the actual footage, just this still.

Then the DS went on to mention that when I was kicked out of the ground, I met up with Mark G who tucked my shirt in for me! The DS asked me was I having a homosexual relationship with Mark; I just chuckled and said are you having a laugh. I knew that the DS wanted to rise me up so I kicked off in the interview, then he would have had me where he wanted.

Basically I told the events as they happened, but at the end of the questioning the DS said he had not heard such bullshit. This reminded me of the Governor at Camp Hill prison when I lost that remission.

Then came the words that hit me like a thunderbolt; "Casellas I hereby charge you with conspiracy to cause violent disorder"

I looked at the Qpr intelligence officer in shock, and fair play to him, he looked shocked too. The DS went on to say I was being refused bail and would be taken straight to court in the morning.

When I was sat in the other room and the DS had gone, the other copper shook his head and said he could not believe what happened. He thought it was going to be a slap on the wrist job; this shit carried a long prison sentence. He even apologized for the behaviour of the DS; anyone would have thought I was being interviewed for an armed robbery or something.

Jan had been waiting outside for me, and I was allowed to see her briefly. Jan said she would come to court in the morning and speak with her brother.

So here I was again, in a police cell worrying my guts out wondering what the outcome of this bollocks would be.

I appeared at West London magistrates the next day and spoke with a duty solicitor. He said he would talk with Jan and see if we could raise a surety for bail. The brief came back and said that Jan's brother would put up £5000 as a surety. This would mean that if I did get bail, I would have to appear back and not get in any further trouble. I was not building my hopes up on this one, as the DS was in court and would try his hardest for me to be remanded.

To my disbelief I was granted bail, and the court would have to wait for the correct paperwork to be received for the surety before I could be released.

I sat in that cell downstairs for what seemed an eternity, and still no sign of the go-ahead to be let out. Another hour went by and the cell door clunked open.

"Bad news I'm afraid, your surety has still not come through, you'll have to get on the van to Wandsworth" explained the security guard.

Now here was an experience I kept telling myself I would never go through again! Sitting in the cramped cubicle on a sweatbox going to HMP Wandsworth, what a life!

I went through all the usual rigmarole of going through reception and taken up to a cell on the remand wing. Oh well at least I would be let out first thing in the morning, or so I thought.

The next morning, we were let out to collect breakfast in our plastic Tupperware and cutlery. Porridge as usual and an overcooked miniature sausage, rasher of bacon and bullet like baked beans. To wash that all down was a cup of steaming tea which tasted like dishwater.

I was expecting the cell door to burst open with the news that the surety had come through and I would be getting out of here. The minutes ticked by in slow motion and the wait went on.

Around 11am the door opened;

"Yes!" I cheered to myself.

"Exercise" chirped the screw

"Bollocks!" I was well gutted; freedom was not beckoning just yet.

Oh well I may as well go on exercise just to get out of this stinking pit I told myself.

Wandsworth prison is one of the oldest nicks in London, the wings all spur off from each other in a star shape with the "centre" obviously in the middle of them all. The centre was the main hub and viewing point for the screws. And just like back in 1990 we had to walk round the centre on the outside either clockwise or anticlockwise; I can't quite remember.

We were led out to an exercise yard and same again we had to march round the outside in a clockwise fashion.

Someone came legging it over and seemed very pleased to see me. Would you believe it; it was Mark G who had been remanded for the trouble at Fulham. Mark had been charged with Conspiracy as well.

We had a chat about the bullshit charge and I explained to Mark I was waiting to get out on bail. He obviously was a bit gutted; it always makes things a bit easier when you know someone when you're inside.

I was now starting to think that Jan's brother could not put up the surety and I would end up banged up here until the case came up. We went back to our cells, and next on the agenda would be lunch.

Just before lunch, the door opened and then came the news I had been itching for;

"Get your kit together Casellas, you're being released on bail!"

I wanted to punch the air and do a jig right there. I said my goodbyes to my cell mate and out I was.

I walked down in the mid morning sunshine to Earlsfield train station and got the next service back to Waterloo. I rang Jan from my mobile with the good news and I met up with her after she had finished work for a pint to celebrate.

A lot of fans had been nicked for the Fulham affair, and a lot of them had already been dealt with and sentenced. That left four of us to appear together at Marylebone Magistrates.

I went to see a barrister at the Chambers up at Chancery Lane in London, they had been recommended to me as they had dealt with football cases before.

The brief was straight with me and said I should plead guilty to a lesser charge. The CCTV footage showed me being aggressive which to be fair he was right. At first I thought I was being stitched up; but then the brief said they would make a bargain with the court that if I went guilty to a charge of Threatening Behaviour, would they drop the conspiracy charge. I decided to go along with that.

Finally the day came for the case to be heard, there was four of us, the two Marks, Tony and myself.

Mark G had his case thrown out due to lack of evidence, and rightly so. Mark had spent six months on remand for nothing.

Tony pleaded not guilty; my memory does not serve me well, so I cannot remember the outcome. The other Mark got a light sentence.

The courts agreed to drop the conspiracy charge on all of us and I got another banning order and big fine.

A load of us went to a nearby pub after to celebrate, as we were all looking at getting years for the concocted charge. Some of the lads who had already been sentenced were there and it was like a home game.

I ended up getting an E off one of the lads and was totally out of the game for the rest of the afternoon. I had not taken an E for a good while now, maybe not the best of ideas in the circumstances!

Not too long after this case I decided to set up my own painting business. I was a good painter and came to the conclusion, why should I keep earning money for someone else, when I was capable of reaping the rewards.

Computers and PC's were now becoming a part of people's lives, and so I bought a package of PC, Printer and scanner. I went on a basic computer literacy course at an Adult college in Catford. That taught me how to use Word and Emails; all I really needed to run my business.

I managed to get in with a big concrete repairs company who worked on big tower blocks and council estates and schools all around the South of England.

I was asked to price up the external painting of two big tower blocks just by Battersea Bridge. They had fixed mast climbers to the side of the towers that went up about nineteen floors. We had to climb off the climbers into balconies on each floor. It was hairy to say the least; three of my mates did not want to work, the heights were too much for them!

I had other jobs on the go, so I had about ten painters working for me at the time. I learned how to pay subcontractor tax for everyone and got myself an accountant. I registered as a Limited company with companies house.

My Limited Company venture did not last long when my accountant asked me how mush I was paying myself. When I explained as much as I needed, he nearly fell over and told me the ins and outs of having a Limited Company. That put me right off, and luckily I was not in too deep so reverted back to being a sole trader business.

Another job I was asked to price for was a school down in Brighton. At first I used to drive every day down there, and my best pal Mart came with me. We got another lad from Butts Farm where Mart was now living to come with us.

After a week of the driving back and forth, we decided to stay in a B and B in Hove and go straight to work from there.

It was obvious what was going to happen, the lure of the pub every night was too much.

It all started well enough, myself and Mart would go back have a shower and then go out for an evening meal and a couple of pints.

Then one of the nights we ended up going down West Street and ended up on a bit of a bender; we went to a few pubs and then to a side street basement bar.

I started acting like a twat and the bouncers chucked me out of the establishment. Just like my usual behaviour I was having none of this and just down the alleyway of the bar there was a building site. I found a long scaffold pole lying on the ground and stomped back to the entrance and started hammering away at the door with the pole. I was shouting at the security to come out and fight.

They either didn't want the aggro or thought I was a loon as they stayed inside. Mart later told me that they had found him and asked him to come out and calm me down and get me away from there.

It was a good job no one saw me from the school we was working on, I was supposed to be a sensible business owner employing painters carrying out contract work!

That was one incident while we were in Brighton, the other mad one came when another night we decided to go to the arches by the beach. There were nightclubs open down there nearly every night and again we decided to get on one in one of the dingy clubs. It was like we were treating this working away lark as a holiday.

The club we went to was decent, good music and plenty of people getting off their heads.

It was like the old raving days and I ended up dancing with a tall blond with a great figure and large boobs. I don't remember her name but she offered to get us some E's. Obviously we did not say no; and the E we had was huge about the size of an old 50p piece.

It didn't take long to take effect and I started to get quite fresh with the girl.

Then a crazy thing happened, I went to the gents had a pee and as I came out of the toilet one of the bouncer approached me. At first I thought he was going to pull me for being too off my face when he asked me did I know what I was doing.

The fella then went on to tell me that the blonde girl had been getting close to was previously a man and had recently undergone the sex change. I explained this to Mart and he was now very curious to say the least. Instead of being put off and running a mile we both questioned the girl on what we had been told.

We were all so out of it on this gigantic E that it was a no holds barred situation. We talked her into going back to her place and we wanted to see how good the "sex change" was!

When we got back to her flat there was already a couple of Gay lads living there and they kind of protected her and stopped us from taking a look at the new genitals; which in hindsight was probably for the best.

All of that happened within a week, never a dull

moment working with Dave! Oh and Mart's Ford Mondeo broke down going back home, we had to wait hours for a breakdown recovery. Mart had only just recently had the motor fixed at a garage in Feltham.

That became another situation, we had to use strong arm tactics shall we say to get Mart's money back, that is another story.

I used to enjoy running my painting business, although to be honest I was not entirely professional enough. The jobs I did for the concrete repair company were all on a contract, and I ended up losing money due to minor clauses. I also did not take out time enough to employ the right painters and came unstuck a few times having to put right shoddy work.

Overall I felt on a high, the money I had coming in was enough, but if I had screwed my loaf a bit more I could have done so much better. I was always more interested in the booze and although I could not see it, that got in the way of my success.
My sister Fran had moved down to Dorset back in the early 1990's, and had got married.

My sister's wedding had been a bit of a disaster all round for her. The fatal mistake had been inviting both mum and Dad; although not together.

My mother had created a terrible scene at the reception; she had screamed at my father who was with Lynn his second wife at the time. I am sure mum had never been able to let go of losing Dad. It was embarrassing enough for me, let alone my sis. At least I melted away into the crowd, got pissed and left early to go back to London with a girlfriend who I had gone with.

Prior to the wedding, sis had an argument with her husband to be and he had pushed her down some stairs which resulted in her arm being in plaster for the wedding.

The final catastrophe was that it absolutely hammered down with rain on the day and all the wedding photos had to be taken inside the church. And then the reception everyone was crammed inside; leading to my mum's angry outburst toward Dad.

I never really forgave my sister's hubby for breaking her arm, and she had to plead with me to not come down and tear him apart.

So fast-forwarding to years later; it was my sister's birthday and her hubby and his family had planned a surprise party in their local pub. The local pub was in West Moors, Dorset; I had been there a few times and got on well with everyone there.

I went down there without Jan and in my mind I was treating this like a mini holiday away from home.

All I did while I was at my sister's was drink can after can of Stella. The weather was good, it was August, and I had a good laugh with her kids playing football in the garden.

On the day of the planned surprise party, sis's hubby's brother came over and asked if I wanted to go into Bournemouth for the day. He even said he was getting some E's; what a day this was going to be!

We started off in a local pub in Ferndown, that is when we dropped the E. I remember us being driven into Bournemouth and going in a big bar which was rammed with holiday makers.

There was a crowd of West Ham fans and I was making a right nuisance of myself but all in good spirits. The E I had taken had kicked in and I was totally off my nut. I went up to the bar and ordered a big round of drinks, I had to have the glasses all put on a tray, and it was fairly heavy.

The inevitable happened, as I squeezed my way through the crowd I dropped the tray, glasses and alcohol flew and crashed everywhere.

The bouncers got hold of me and tried chucking me out; of course I wasn't going peacefully. The lad I was with stepped in and calmed me down and assured the security he was taking me home.

There was no way I was going back to my Sis's I was having a whale of a time causing carnage!

What I didn't know at the time was that the poor lad had to make a call to my sis to warn her what was going on. My sis then rang Mart and asked what to do with me, as I was running riot.

In the end I was driven to a Holiday Inn, and suggested I take a rest and calm down. How can someone take a rest and slow down when in the full flow of effects from a very strong E.

Mart had suggested to my sis to just let me get on with it; he knew me well, but she ignored the advice. My sis was still unaware of her surprise party in the pub; all she knew was she was going out for a few drinks. My sis also knew what I was capable of and just wanted me out of the way.

It was totally mad, I had no idea where I was, but I did just about remember the name of the pub for my sis's party. There was no way I was missing out on that. I had only been at the hotel for about an hour, I asked the bloke on reception to call me a cab to get to the pub. He had been asked to make sure I did not leave, but what could he do, I was not a prisoner.

I was still completely off my face and the cab driver was probably relieved to offload me at the pub. I had left my trainers at the hotel so I was in just my socks; which I was unaware of at the time.

When I entered the pub, the surprise party was in full swing. I made a dramatic entrance and was shouting at my sis for abandoning me like that. After a few minutes of a slanging match, my Sis's husband Ian finally persuaded me to go home. Ian took me back to my car, which was parked outside their house. Ian asked me to stay in the car and get some sleep and work off the effects of the E and all the booze I had drank.

I lay in the back of my Sierra and blasted out tunes on the car stereo. Finally I must have nodded off for a few hours. When I woke up I had a mouth like sandpaper and felt very rough. I still felt under the effects of the pill though, so certainly has not worked it all off.

I felt very aggrieved that Ian and my sis had made me stay in the motor, so I went all guns blazing to knock on the front door.

Sis told me to go away and go back to sleep; she was furious I had ruined her party and made a total dick of us both.

I asked to speak to Ian; she told me he was not letting me into the house. That's when I lost the plot, I said I was going to kill him, maybe I thought I owed him one for breaking her arm before their wedding. Ian ran through the house and out to the back garden to get away from me.

The front door had a semi-circle of toughened glass panels at the top. I punched one through with my right fist and then a second one with my left. All I saw then was blood spurting out of my right wrist and blood dripping from my left. This freaked me and I pleaded to be let in as I was in trouble. My sis told me to "Fuck off and die"; I really thought my time was up; blood was all over the place.

One of sis's friends appeared and came out, she told me to sit down and hold my arms up in the air to slow down the flow of blood.

My luck must have been in that night, because my sis's friend happened to be a Paramedic that probably saved my life. She called an ambulance and sat with me until it arrived.

After all the aggro that I had caused I decided to go into "loved up" mode. I chatted up the paramedics, who knew my sis's friend, so I was treated with a bit more respect than was deserved.

I was taken to Bournemouth hospital and went straight into A and E. I tried hugging the nurses and asked for kisses, what a mental scenario, I had blood pumping out all over the place. One nurse kept asking me to go and lie down on a trolley and chill out. Eventually I did, and as I lay there I heard something dripping on the floor. When I looked down I could see blood rapidly dripping from my left thumb. The corner off my thumb had been shaved off with the glass; I was in no pain at all I must have been numbed out with all the booze and the E.

I was informed by a doctor that I could not be stitched up that night. Ligaments had been severed in my right wrist and the cut had missed my artery by a millimetre, I had been a lucky boy. I needed to have microsurgery and as this was the bank holiday weekend I would have to wait until Tuesday and go to Salisbury hospital.

I got a cab back to my sisters and was told I had to sleep in the car. Apparently I had scared the life out of my nephew and niece when I had punched the door through. Both my hands were in bandages with blood seeping through. I was so thirsty; I had to knock on the door to ask for a bottle of water.

It was a very uncomfortable night and I hardly slept, eventually the morning came and the sun shone through the windows of the Sierra.

I found my mobile phone in the glove compartment, but I could not find my trainers and I was still in my socks, what must I have looked like; everywhere I had been since the brief stay at the hotel I had been trainer-less.

I rang my sis and assured her I was sober again and asked could I come indoors. Obviously she was very skeptical about letting me in, she told me Ian's father was on his way and wanted to talk to me.

Ian's dad was a born again Christian so I knew he was a decent bloke. I had to face the music, I felt like shit and my hands were in bandages with blood seeping through. My right arm had a splint to stop any movement, what a mess!

I sat very sheepishly at the table in the dining room, had a cup of tea and you could cut the atmosphere with a knife.

Ian's Dad finally arrived and we went out in the garden; it was August Bank Holiday and the sun was beaming down. The heat was frying my head even more than my hangover and come-down from the E.

Ian's Dad said he could not believe where I got the strength from to punch through two toughened glass panels. He went on to talk about God and how he forgave me; he placed his hands on top of my head and said a blessing.

At first I thought this was all a load of crap and a wind up; but he was serious and this kind of humbled me.

Ian's Dad did not stay long, and after he had left my Sis told me I could not stay there for the night. I had an appointment for surgery at Salisbury hospital the next day; so I rang Mart and asked could he get the train up to Bournemouth. The way my hands were I could not drive, so Sis said she would drive me to Bournemouth and Ian would follow and take her back in their car.

I could always rely on my best pal Mart to get me out of the shit, and I agreed to pay for his fare and for the night in a B and B.

10 TIME TO WAKE UP

I had been speaking to Jan and after this latest shenanigan, we came to the conclusion I had to stop drinking. This was the first time I had ever admitted that alcohol was a problem, and Jan gave me an ultimatum, the booze or her and our marriage.

On a hot day like this all I wanted to do was go and sit in a pub's beer garden and get right back on it. I had to grit my teeth and stay dry, not an easy task.

I met Mart at Bournemouth station where we had parked the car and he drove us to Salisbury. We found a little B and B and then went out for a meal that evening. It was torture not drinking, but I was in the realization I had to start sorting myself out; I had a lot to lose.

The microsurgery the next day was a weird

experience, the surgeon wore what looked like a mini miners torch strapped round his forehead. A tourniquet was strapped tightly round my upper arm to stop any blood flow.

To be fair the surgeon worked wonders, he soldered my ligaments back to together and delicately stitched me back up. Then came a few moments of excruciating pain, when the tourniquet was taken off, all the blood rushed down my arm like a tidal wave of pressure. At least it was over quickly.

Mart drove me back to Catford; he had done me a right favour. It had only been a few months before this that I had driven to the Isle of Sheppey to collect from his release from prison. That is another story which is personal to Mart.

It had been a long time since myself and Jan had a serious conversation, and I agreed to start some counselling around my drinking and my childhood which had a lot to do with my drunken rage. I had an assessment and agreed to attend the weekly sessions.

In the meantime Jan still continued to drink up to two bottles of wine every night and a spliff. I must admit this did bother me, and when we went out we still went to the pub. When I sat in the pub all I could focus on was what everyone else was drinking and I would stare at the amber liquid in drinkers' pint glasses.

Meanwhile at work, I had a few issues with other painters messing up work. And of course I was left to sort it all out and ended up losing money. I decided to call it a day with the contract work and ended up going back to work for an Irish building firm in Peckham.

It was a good old school set-up, the main man Maurice had a lock up and little office in Peckham and he paid every one pound notes on a Friday. We used to queue up at 5pm and get our money; down the road from the yard was a pub called the Wishing Well and a load of us would stay in there for hours.

There was many a time that I would end up drinking on my own all round Peckham High Road and I sometimes ended up in some seriously seedy bars full of black fellas. I would be on my own wearing work clothes covered in paint and start dancing around to the DJ's who were on. In my own way I was trying to prove that white men can dance!

Again I got away with murders in those places and

somehow am still living to tell the tale.

So now I found it harder working with this mob as I wasn't drinking anymore. It was a struggle trying to stay sober but I was gritting my teeth through it.

I found myself spending more time on my computer now I had stopped drinking. I stumbled across a private messaging service from AOL, and it was more like an arena to chat to women.

I started having a bit of fun with a woman up in Leeds, she asked for me to send a pic, which I did. She sent a photo of herself and we chatted each other up every night.

One evening I came home from work and Jan was in tears but also fuming at the same time.

Jan took me to the computer, opened up the screen and showed me the dialogue I had been having with the girl from Leeds.

I had left my passwords and log-ins on a pad on the desk, so it had been easy for Jan to see what had been going on.

We had a blazing row, and it was almost as if this was the moment I needed as an excuse to get back on the booze again.

I told Jan I was leaving and packed up some clothes in a couple of sports bags. Jan was distraught, but I was adamant that was it for me.

I got in my car and sped up the road, my first point of call was the off license. I bought a dozen cans of Stella and then I rang up Mart to explain what I had just done.

Good old Mart never let me down and said I could go and stay with him at his house on Butts Farm. It was like a home-coming for me; I was back on the estate where I spent many teenage years and I was now a free man again to do what I wanted. I had been sober for two months, and for me that was more than enough; I had chosen the booze over my marriage, flat, business and everything that I had built up over the years.

Mart lived in a council house with his wife and four kids, and for him to just let me move in like that was an act of generosity I will never forget.

I shared a bedroom with Marts two sons, which they found a great laugh.

I managed to get Steve, Mart's eldest son a job with me painting with the Irish mob. We would walk to Whitton station in the morning and get a train to

Clapham Junction and then onto Thornton Heath where the job was. I was on a crazy mission of self devastation and drank on the job. Steve even joined me and there was another lad from Brixton who was working there. Somehow we got away with our antics as the people that lived in the house we were decorating were down to earth.

One of the evenings after work we went in a pub near Thornton Heath station and had a good few pints; it was pay day and Maurice had dropped off our wages for us.

When we got off the train at Whitton we walked along the A316 a big dual carriage way that ran alongside Butts Farm. As we crossed over the bridge, I stopped and looked down at the rush hour traffic speeding by. I started shouting like a madman and burst in to tears.

Steve asked me what the matter was, I explained I had had enough of life, and I felt like jumping over the bridge in front of a car. Steve pulled me out of it, and we went back and drank some more.

I had been taking loads of E's again when I left Jan, it was like I was on a massive bender and my self will was running riot. The problem was I had not stopped to think about what I had done so my emotions must have built up like a volcano erupting. And that was what I was right now, an explosion of emotion fuelled by alcohol and Ecstasy tablets. When I left Jan it was as though I had given myself a license to rid myself of all responsibility and be a free spirit.

What was free? Free to lose self control that was what I was doing. Mart and his family put up with me, we had known each other since the age of eleven and never judged each other for anything.

Some of my behaviour in Mart's home was unacceptable, I stayed there for many months before I started to get it together to look for somewhere to rent.

I saw an advert in a local shop for a room to rent on the Beavers Estate in Hounslow, up near Heathrow airport.

I went to see the lady whose house it was; she was a young Irish woman and was already renting out her other bedroom. She seemed very friendly and welcoming and showed me the room; it was a fair size, all I needed really. All I had was a TV and my clothing so it was easy to move all my stuff out of Mart's.

I was still popping E's like boiled sweets and drinking throughout the day. I was still working; painting and I now had a motor to drive around in.

Hounslow wasn't really my manor so I spent most of my time around Whitton and Twickenham. I was carrying around so many E's that if I had of been nicked or stop searched I could have got years inside.

I was shagging around loads of women, and none of it meant anything. I had never really stopped to feel any grief of throwing my marriage away; I just drowned and numbed it all out.

There was some nights when I lay in my bed in that room and burst into tears, and in my madness I would take another E to see if that settled me down and got me to sleep. I had outer body experiences of myself rising out of my body and looking down on myself on the bed.

I also had what felt like electric shocks going through my brain; it was very scary and felt like I was going to die.

It was not so obvious at the time but the combination of the pills and excessive alcohol abuse were taking a physical effect on my brain.

It was now 2001 and my banning order for the Fulham incident was coming to an end thankfully. QPR had just played a pre-season tournament in Ibiza and I could not go. I had to hand in my passport for the duration of the series of matches and every time we played I had to sign in at Hounslow police station. This was a complete pain the arse; and ironically I wanted my team to be knocked out of the tournament so I didn't have to keep going back and forth to the old bill shop. We went on to win the tournament and apparently when we played Coventry in the final it had kicked off left right and centre and all the lads had a blinding time out there.

The first game that came up when my ban ended was Crewe away and there was a coach load of all the old faces going from O'Donaghues pub in Shepherds Bush.

Myself, Mart and Kev decided to get an early bus up there. I had been out all night and had been on the snort so felt like absolute shit. The pub was open early for breakfasts and I could not face any food. I had another pint and ended up outside the boozer chucking up all over the pavement just as some of the older lads were arriving.

It was great to be back! The coach was full of fifty of

our top lads and the journey up was a good laugh, reminiscing and generally getting on the booze and coke again.

By the time we arrived in Crewe I was in a right state, we went in a pub near the station which was already full of other QPR lads.

This was only my first game back and already I was buzzing to see my team in action again. We didn't all head to the ground together, myself, Mart and Kev walked up and I still had a bottle of beer in my hand.

As we approached the ground a woman copper rushed over to me and told me to put the bottle in a bin, I argued that I wanted to finish it. Mart convinced me to go back and find a bin, I was now in one of those moods where I was way over excited and could not let things go.

The other lads entered in the ground after a small queue, I must have looked a lot worse than I felt because a Crewe steward came over and informed me he was not letting me into the stadium.

I began arguing my defense and I was told I was too drunk to enter. I pleaded that I had come all this way on a coach and spent money and this was out of order. The Steward was adamant and as I walked away from him I turned and called him a Northern cunt.

That was the cue for two PC's one was the same WPC who approached me earlier. I was nicked and taken to the Old bill station, I was so pissed I was thrown in a cell and crashed out straight away.

I was out for the count for about three hours when the cell door opened; and I awoke to the marvelous sight of a very nice blonde WPC. She had a massive grin on her face and said it was time for me to get my belongings and get out of here. As we walked back to the sergeant's desk, my head was banging.

The WPC asked me to say "Cockney geezer!" I didn't know if she was taking the piss out of me; I said it anyway. This was all very surreal, here I was in a cop shop in Crewe and I had a stunning police officer asking me to talk in my London accent to her. She asked me to repeat it to another good looking WPC and they both chuckled. I was starting to enjoy being here in this stinking police station; that was a first for me!

As I was being given my mobile phone, cash and keys back I heard a very familiar voice. It was JK; he had been on the coach this morning. JK had been nicked after the game and told me there had been a bit of a row with some cocky Crewe lads.

It was very dark outside by now and we had to find our way back to the station. We found out there was no direct train back to London and we had to go to Birmingham New Street first. Back at Birmingham we then found out there was maintenance work being carried out on the line back to Euston. Again we had to change and get a rail service coach back to Heathrow. What a shit night this was, been nicked again at football and can't even get home. At least I had JK as my companion on this journey from hell.

We had to appear back at Crewe Magistrates a few weeks later; JK had his case thrown out, I pleaded guilty to being drunk while entering a football ground. I got another three year ban; would I ever watch my beloved Qpr again!?" My life now consisted of scratching around for work and when I had the money I would just pay my rent for the room and get wasted on booze and E's.

I found myself in meaningless flings with various women although it all seemed good at the time.

The lady whose house I lived in sat me down one morning at her kitchen table. She had heard me crying some nights in my room and the drunken sessions with the girls I bought back. I just came and went and never really socialized with this kind lady or the other fella that lived in the other room.

I felt too paranoid to have any contact and just avoided any face to face interaction whatsoever.

My landlady phoned a friend and asked me to speak to him; it turned out he was a substance abuse counsellor or something like that. He sounded very understanding and asked if I wanted any help. I turned down the offer of support and just said I would give it a thought.

I was knocking around with a lad who had just come out of prison and was living in a parole/bail hostel in Richmond. His name was also Martin; we bonded straight away and ended up getting pissed as long as we could afford it. There was a good old character that lived up in the attic flat in the hostel. The old boy had a few birds in a cage that would sing and make a racket. He was definitely the bird man of Richmond.

A couple of times I had crashed out on Martins floor in his room and we went up to see the bird man first thing in the morning. He was in a right mess and had alcoholic fits and we would have to leg it down the local shop and get him a couple of cans of super to snap him out of his seizure. It was scary stuff seeing someone like that and very tragic.

Martin would come over and stay in my room in Hounslow and we would end up all night listening to my CD's and getting on the E's.

I was taking a real risk, I would be walking round with large quantities of E's on my possession; they would never last long though!

I managed to get hold of a Ford Sierra 2litre GLS for £200 an absolute bargain. I would drive round banging out the tunes and act a bit like a boy racer.

One morning after a long drinking session, we woke up in my room and the landlady made us a quality fry-up. I didn't feel so paranoid when I had someone with me and was able to face this kind lady.

I had been looking for somewhere else to live and my mates Joe and Tiz had agreed to let me come and live in a house they were renting in Whitton.

I was in the process of moving there and had bagged up all my worldly possessions into a few black bin liners. The black bags were in the boot of my Sierra. The lock on the boot was missing and there was just a hole where it should have been. I was able to unclick the lock mechanism using a flat head screwdriver and kept the tool on the dashboard.

Myself and Martin had finished our cooked breakfast and decided to head over to Teddington to see a girl we were knocking around with and get back on the booze again.

We stopped at a corner shop bought some cans, Mart sat in the passenger side swigging away.

As we drove through Twickenham, we came to the traffic lights right by the Cabbage Patch pub and there was a lone copper standing just by the lights on the left.

Just my luck the lights turned red; I said to Martin to keep the can of lager down and do not look at the officer of law.

What did Martin do? Yes you guessed it he stared straight at our uniformed friend and carried on gulping back on his beer.

The PC did not look impressed and pointed at me to pull over.

"For fuck sake Martin, what did I say" I barked at

my brainless pal.

I pulled in just round from the lights and got out the car.

The officer walked round my Sierra shaking his head and got on his radio immediately.

Twickenham Police station was literally just up the road and it wouldn't be long before back-up arrived.

The usual questioning ensued;

"Is this you car sir?"

"Why is there no lock in the boot; please open it up for me"

Then the copper took one look at the black bags and put two and two together; he suspected we had just committed a burglary and had taken the car.

I had only just bought this motor and the new log book had not been sent off yet.

Then to make matters worse I was asked to give a breath sample.

"Bollocks!" I thought to myself; I had been drinking all night, surely I was way over the limit. Martin hadn't helped by blatantly waving his can of Stella at our friendly law enforcer!

I blew into the breathalyser as directed and waited for the inevitable bad news.

"This must be your lucky day; the reading is under the limit"

What a result that was! The breakfast I had eaten an hour before must have soaked up a lot of the booze from the night before and saved my bacon. Literally!

A police van pulled over from across the road, and I was being arrested for suspicion of burglary and taking a vehicle.

Martin was let away and off he went happy as Larry to go to Teddington to continue his merry drinking. I was left right in the shit and ended up banged up in a cell early in the morning.

The geezer I had bought the car from verified I was the new owner; and I explained I was in the process of moving my belongings to a new address.

Eventually I was let out late afternoon and given the keys back for my Sierra.

That was one incident; the next one came along

about a week later. I had lent the motor to Mart my best pal as he was seeing someone over in Chertsey and went over there for the evening.

When Mart came back in the morning, the back window of the Sierra was smashed out!

There had been a big argument and someone had put a brick through my window. Mart managed to get the bill paid for a new window on a credit card owned by his friend who had seen the night before.

To be honest I did not really like staying with Joe and the others in Whitton, I was sleeping on the floor of a little box room and I was always hung over or on a come down from the E's.

We did have some good times though, some great after pub parties and long nights of being off our nuts.

I was now working; window cleaning with Joe and his brother who had a massive round all round Richmond. I also did a few little painting jobs for them which kept me ticking over.

I was pretty much running riot, I had mates in Hounslow, Teddington, Whitton and Richmond. There was always someone to get on a session with. And there was always a female about to have a good time with, I always had unprotected sex and somehow got away with never getting a girl pregnant or not getting an STD.

I had a mad experience when I rang up to insure the Sierra; I spoke to a young woman on the phone and we got talking about the music I had on the CD player.

I gave all my details and my mobile number for the car insurance records. About ten minutes later the girl who dealt with the insurance rang me back. She said that she loved the trance music too and that I sounded nice. We arranged to meet up one day in Peterborough. This was where she lived and I was certain that she was married as I had to meet her well down the road from her house. She said it was her parents house and she did not want them knowing. I would say she was in her mid twenties, and it seemed strange that she was still at her mum and dads, who knew!?

I drove back and forth up the A1 every few weeks and we went out to the bars in Peterborough. A mate of mine, Jason came a few times and we had some top nights out.

There was one night when I fancied going up to Peterborough; it was a spur of the moment decision. It was about 3am and I had been drinking all day and was really in no shape to drive. I had about three hours sleep and got in my Sierra and started the drive up to Heathrow and then round the M25 toward the junction for the A1.

I was so tired, what I did not realize was that I had taken the turn for the M1 and not the A1. Somehow I came off one of the junctions and got back on track again.

This journey seemed endless and I eventually hit the A1 again. I must have got about half way up when all of a sudden I awoke with an HGV driver to my left in the middle land sounding the trucks' horn. The lorry driver looked at me as if to say are you OK and put his thumbs up at me. I had been in the fast lane and must have nodded off at the steering wheel and if it had not been for that fella I would probably be dead now.

That shook me right up and I came off at the next slip road and found a residential area and climbed into the back seats and had a sleep for a few hours.

Even though that was a near death experience; it still didn't prompt me to address my issues with substance abuse. I just carried on in a meaningless existence. It might sound like I was having the time of my life; I even went to Reading Festival with Joe and load of the other lads; but deep inside I just wasn't happy.

Loads of crazy things happened at Reading, and I was so out of it I did not even watch one band or go to any of the stages. The first night I was there a few of us went in a rave tent; I got E'd up and the rest of the four days and nights were just a blur.

I was living with Mikey and his wife and kids; he had kindly let me stay with him as long as I kept things under control. When I got back from Reading; Mikey took a photo of me in his garden. I did not like what I saw; I was a mess and in my eyes I started to look like a haunted man.

I upset Mikey a few times while living with him; one night I was locked out and tried climbing in through windows in his conservatory at the back. I woke everyone up and we nearly came to blows yet again.

Then there was the day that I took Mikey's car and drove round all day on a mission visiting various people and getting on the booze as per usual. To say Mikey was not happy is an understatement.

I started doing a bit of shoplifting again; nicking

bottles of spirits, steaks and other bits and pieces from supermarkets.

I still went up to Peterborough every now and then; and there was a lad Pete who I became a mate with. We came up with this crazy idea to go and live in Faliraki. I suggested this as I remembered how much I loved the place when I went on holiday back in 1998 with Jan. And I had just been out there for a week with another fella Mel and while we were out there I got talking to a small English employment agency who said it would be easy to get a little job out there.

11. FALIRAKI

Myself and Peter booked a week's holiday and then planned on getting some work off the agency and just stay there indefinitely.

The first night we arrived in Faliraki we just went for it. There was a stripper's bar and we headed there; we were already well steaming on the booze.

We took our seats and enjoyed the sights on offer. Then we were approached by a couple of stunning Russian girls who were obviously Lap dancers. They offered for us to go to a room at the back of the bar. At first I declined but then thought "Fuck it lets just go for it".

I said to Peter I would put my credit card behind the bar to pay for our time with these two stunners.

I had no idea how much credit I had left on the card. I had been using the card to draw cash out and had paid for the holiday and new clothes. It didn't matter to me as I had lost all care of responsibility in the last few years since leaving Jan.

We were both round the back for a good half an hour and I kept racking up the bill. When we eventually went back round to the bar, the Greek barman asked me how I was going to pay the bill.

I explained back to the big lump of a bar manager that they had my credit card and to take payment out of that.

Then came another bombshell; I was told that I had run out of credit and now I had no money to pay the rest of the bill.

We had been here just one night and I was already skint. Pete had a bit of money but not enough to throw away on the lap dancers.

Basically I had to put my hands up and say I could not settle the bill. The big fella was a typical Greek with open shirt and long dark pony tail hanging down his back. I remembered back to my holiday in 1998 and to when one of the bar owners showed me an automatic pistol. He told me that when there was any trouble with US navy on shore leave he would just pull his gun and get rid of them!

The manager was adamant that I leave my passport

with him until the bill got paid. I kind of chuckled and retorted that I was staying here in Faliraki for good and that he could keep my passport!

When we got back to the hotel the owner there already knew about our antics at the strip bar. It was apparent that everyone knew each other here or was related in some way.

There was probably some kind of Greek MAFIA that owned most of the clubs and bars and there was no getting away with this one. In any case they had my passport so I was going nowhere; which was our intentions anyway.

The hotel boss explained who owned the strip bar and told us we could go and speak with him at his bar/nightclub the next day.

Faliraki has two main streets, bar street and club street and at night during the holiday season is packed with large groups getting on the cocktails and generally getting paralytic.

The Greek authorities were getting fed up with drunken bodies lying everywhere and young holidaymakers disrespecting the local area. A few times I saw the army wading into lads with their batons. It was just as well I had hardly any money or

I could have been right in trouble.

One of the reasons I came with Pete to Faliraki was to start a new life and get myself off the Ecstasy pills.

This was not exactly a sane choice of places to retreat to for drug rehabilitation!

The owner of the strip bar was called Charlie; he was a short stocky fella and even looked like a MAFIA boss.

He was very approachable and thought the whole affair of not being able to settle my lap dancer bill was hilarious.

Charlie gave me my passport back straight away and asked me a bit about myself.

I told him I was a painter and decorator and his eyes lit up. He came to a deal that if I painted his office above his nightclub and another office he had; he would let me off the money I owed him.

During the day both Pete and myself had got some work through the agency; I was doing some painting for a watersports company and Pete got a little job fixing the go-carts at the local track.

The Watersports firm was called Sotos and Akis that

was the brothers' names who ran the banana boats and ringos down on the beach. They had bought a salvaged German schooner that had sunk off the local coast. Their plan was to renovate the schooner and then take holidaymakers out on booze cruises.

The schooner was moored up off the main beach; it was a lovely vessel and had a very tall mast which was made of metal. Sotos wanted me to paint the mast and make it have a wood effect. I had to use two part paint; a base coat and then using a comb for the finish coat would give a wood grain effect.

Every day the sun beat down on this old fishing town, the good weather was guaranteed. The year was 2002 and we were here during the World Cup. It was exactly four years after I had come on holiday with Jan.

Pete got away from the go-carts for a couple of days to help me with the mast. Sotos took us out to the ship in a speedboat and dropped us off with the materials we needed. We were given a couple of bottles of water and Sotos said he would come back at lunchtime with a Greek salad each.

The mast had a bosuns chair attached to a pulley and rope. My job was to climb in the chair and Pete would haul me up section by section. I had to balance a pot of paint and brush at the same time as applying the base coat; not an easy task.

The sun was fierce and I was frying up there; to make things even more difficult a big speedboat being driven by a Greek who had tourists on board kept circling the schooner. This created waves and the ship rocked back and forth; I was hanging on for dear life. The Greek in the speedboat kept roaring with laughter. At first I did not clock on to what was happening; it was later that Sotos told us that the speedboat belonged to a rival watersports crew and they were trying to sabotage our efforts out of envy.

We came back the next day and finished the mast; and on this day England were playing one of the group matches. I was right up the top of the mast when there was a roar; it sounded like a jet plane had flew over my head. Yet there was no sign of any aircraft; I realized later that it was when England scored the cheer from the packed bars had created the sound of an aircraft!

Sotos and Akis decided it would be better to get the schooner round to a more secluded bay and moor it up there. They then wanted all the decks sanded, caulked and varnished. That was my next job; Pete went back to the go-carts.

We rented a poky little room for five Euros each a night which was above a shop in bar street; it was ok just to get our heads down and have a shower.

I got another little job after the painting on the schooner was finished getting people into a shitty bar just away from the main streets. I was quite good at encouraging groups of lads in but the stingy owner hardly ever gave me any free drinks which pissed me off.

The longer I was in Faliraki the less money I had for drinking and I decided to get back to London again. My good pal Joe wired over the money for a flight back to Heathrow and I went back to stay at Mikey's house.

Pete stayed out in Faliraki and to this day I do not know whatever happened in his life.

My plan of starting a new life did not work but at least I was off the E's so that was a bonus. I managed to keep away from the pills and decided to move out of Mikey's and the only room I could find was above the Kings Arms pub in Teddington High Street.

A couple of old friends already lived above the pub and it all started off great there. I was shagging a couple of women and really living the bachelor lifestyle. The downfall was that the bar was right under my room and temptation was right there.

The owners of the pub were right on the cocaine and obviously loved the booze. I started getting on the coke myself and things started to get messy again.

I now had a job working for a small painting outfit which a mate had recommended me to.

I never really let drinking get in the way of my daily work all these years; I used to wait until the day was over.

But the fact that the pub was one road away from the house I was painting became all too easy for me. I would go for a lunch break and end staying there way too long and go back to the job half pissed. And all the time I was running up a bar bill; by the time I got my cheque for the painting most of it went on the rent for room in the pub and the beer debt.

I thought everything was ok at the job; the lady seemed happy with my work and I only really ever saw her when she came in sometimes herself for lunch.

Then on the second week of the job I went to meet the boss and his right hand man at the property. It was a Friday and I was looking forward to getting my cheque as usual.

The governor looked at me and dropped the bombshell; "Sorry Dave we don't have any more work for next week, I have to lay you off"

I had been layed off a few times before and just took it on the chin. What did seem strange though was that the job hadn't been finished.

Well that was that, I headed back up the road to the pub and drowned my sorrows.

Later that evening my mate who put me on to the job came in the Kings Arms. He told me that the boss didn't want to upset me or get into any argument. The lady whose house it was had complained that I was taking long lunches and smelled of alcohol whenever she saw me.

This was the first time in my life I had lost a job due to my drinking; I had always been OK, but as I said I never mixed work and drinking before, so was this a wake up call?

I now had my tail between my legs and was feeling very sorry for myself. It was not enough to prompt me to do anything about my boozing though; it just meant I was in a bit of bother as I had no money coming in to pay for my room at the pub.

I started selling a few bits and pieces and at the weekends there would be a small crowd at the bar coming in to see me. The governors of the pub were not stupid and realized what was going on. I got a severe warning and told if I didn't pack it in I would be evicted.

That was rich coming from two of the most powder snorting individuals I knew!

It was time to get out of the pub; it wasn't going to be easy with no money to find another room to rent.

A mate of mine Simon lived on his own in a flat the other side of Teddington and I kept at him to let me stay there until I could sort myself out.

I promised I would behave and not take the piss at his place. We were both very similar in that we loved our booze and both of us had "mental issues!"

We had a good laugh living together although Simon got overly paranoid about things and we ended up clashing. I broke my promise and bought back women while he was at work.

I really had to start doing something to get out of the mess I was in. I went to my doctor and asked what help I could get about my drinking and he referred me to Richmond alcohol services.

While I was at my docs I explained about my chaotic housing situation and he pointed me to a homeless organization in Richmond. In the meantime I was still seeing Andy my counsellor at the alcohol support service. Andy mentioned about the homeless place as well; so I went along to see them too. The organization was called SPEAR and they did an assessment with me and I told them I was also seeing Andy once a week to try and sort out my drinking and substance abuse.

SPEAR told me that there was a long waiting list for their night shelter just off Richmond roundabout but to keep checking in.

12. TAKING ACTION

I was trying my hardest to be as honest as I could with Andy in my weekly sessions. It was more of a support service than actual counselling. Although I had told Andy all about my upbringing and my life so far.

There was still a big part of me that could never see myself stopping drinking. The other stuff like the E's and coke I could really take it or leave it. Booze was biggest addiction; I had got pissed since the age of fourteen and it was my best friend.

While I was still at Simon's we both agreed that we would try and get off the drink at the same time. After hours and hours of contemplating I finally agreed to go into a residential rehabilitation centre up near Reading.

Andy had fought my corner at the alcohol service and secured funding for the rehab.

I went up on a train with a girlfriend of mine; she kind of held my hand all the way as there was no way I could face it on my own.

The rehab centre was an old manor house and was in fact called Yeldhall Manor. There were stunning grounds all around and a little farm. It looked like most of the veg was grown there too.

Yeldhall was a Christian based establishment and part of the treatment would involve attending Alcoholics Anonymous meetings and working the 12-steps of AA.

I met the main man there and he seemed very welcoming and genuinely wanted me to succeed. I met other lads there while they were having lunch in what looked like a banqueting room.

Some of the fellas were fresh out of prison and they seemed at peace with themselves and spoke of a higher power.

The first eight weeks I would have to share with a room mate. The whole treatment would last eleven months; and there was a system where I would move on to different stages and eventually be placed in a small studio flat in the grounds depending on how the treatment had gone.

I shook the boss's hand and agreed to the eleven months. The catch was that I had to be sober from day one; and I made a commitment to detox myself at Simon's.

I felt fairly positive about all this; but also very scared at the same time.

I had got to a point in my life where I was always totally anxious when I was sober and found it very hard being around people unless I'd had a few drinks.

Andy got me a prescription for Zopiclone sleeping tablets to help me through the self detox. It would take two weeks of climbing the walls and then off to start rehab.

Simon also managed to get hold of sleepers as well. We would play Trivial Pursuit then neck half of a sleeper and be asleep within half an hour!

My lifestyle up until now had been what a lot of fellas would only dream about. I had been seeing two women at the same time, they were mates and we would have threesomes. The downside was that I was always out of it; too drunk to really enjoy what was going on. Of course I loved it, but my head was way too messed up to appreciate anything good in my life.

Most of my mates and the two girls were proud of my decision to get sober and clean; but was I really 100% proud of myself.

The two weeks of drying out were over; it was the day that was going to change my life forever.

I had done all the hard work of keeping off the alcohol but there was a voice in my head telling me I could not go through with it. The biggest fear I had was to share a room; I had done that many times in prison before. But this was voluntary; I had no choice before.

The morning was here for me to go get the train to Yeldhall Manor. I picked up my mobile phone and made the call.

I told them I could not do it, I wasn't coming and sorry for messing about.

The boss was cool as a cucumber; he told me I was not the first person to get itchy feet and he wished me all the very best.

After those two torturous weeks I almost ran to the off license and grabbed four cans of Stella off the shelf.

To say Andy wasn't pleased was an understatement! One thing he thanked me for though was at least I didn't go and start the treatment and then make a run for it. The funding was not lost so that was not such a disaster for them.

I continued to see Andy; and I could tell he was frustrated but he stuck with me and we both kept faith in me.

Things got worse with Simon; I acted like a prick and we fell out big time. I had to find somewhere else to live so I went back to SPEAR in Richmond.

I was lucky as there was a space coming up in the hostel; I filled in a few forms with them and was given a date to move in.

The irony was that I had to share a room with another lad. His name was Les and was a mad Scottish fella with wild hair like Braveheart. Just like me he was always pissed so we got on like a house on fire.

The first morning I awoke and Les was sleeping on the floor. I asked him why he had crashed on the deck and wasn't in his comfortable single bed.

Les had lived on the streets for so long he told me

that beds were too soft for him and the floor was what he was used to.

There is always someone a lot worse off than yourself; although I was so full of my own shit I didn't even see that.

Every morning we could have breakfast but then had to leave the hostel and were allowed to return after 4.00pm.

I was still doing a bit of Window cleaning with Joe; but I was becoming a bit of a nightmare as after a couple of hours all I could think about was getting a drink.

After all those years ago of being ok with working at heights my nervous system was starting to deteriorate as being up ladders started to freak me out a bit.

I had always had a good appetite and ate well; but even my food consumption was rapidly diminishing.

My diet mainly consisted of eating small amounts and loads of booze and if I could get hold of any E's or coke that was all I needed.

There was another girl over in Teddington that I started to hang round with. There would always be other lads all sniffing around as well. We were a typical group of alkies and addicts with one sole purpose; to get smashed as long as the funds allowed.

I won't mention names here but the girl was a tragic example of a very kind individual who totally changed after a couple of drinks. She was a great looker too and I did have a little fling with her and so did other lads.

Most of our days we spent playing loud music; luckily the neighbour was a young lad on methadone who was trying to stay away from using heroin. When I say lucky I mean he was one of us and would never had complained about the noise.

I would go back to the hostel in the evening and basically just get my head down to sleep. One evening I went back and I had taken an E; I sat down in the communal sitting area and began coming up on the pill.

There were a few others all chatting including Les my room mate. As I started to rush from the effects of the E; I began letting everyone know I was enjoying my buzz. For some reason Les began lecturing me on the dangers of drugs and why could I not just enjoy myself on the booze.

That was it; I flew off the handle and began shouting at Les and basically offering him out for a fight.

Just by the residents area was a tiny office that the night staff sat in and monitored the place.

One of the workers came steaming out of the room and told me to go to bed and calm down. I was still fuming and had enough of everything.

I believe I was becoming so impatient with the situation I had found myself in especially with the housing. I had been told that morning that I would have to wait a while before there was any chance of moving on from here.

I was still on prescribed sleeping tablets and what I did next I did not ever see myself doing.

I went up to the room and sat on my bed and looked up at the ceiling in despair. I reached into the drawer of the bedside cabinet and took out the box of Zopiclone. There were around a dozen of the minute blue pills still in the silver packaging.

One by one I popped them all in my mouth and washed them down with a gulp of the bottled water I had on top of the cabinet. I did not even think of any consequences and just lay back on the bed still under the influence of booze and the E.

The next thing that happened was me opening my eyes and not knowing where I was. My head felt like it was going to explode and my mouth was as dry as the Sahara desert. I had a horrible metallic taste in my mouth and I could make out I was in a hospital bed. I was on a drip and in a paper like gowns which are open all the way up my back. I still had my boxer shorts on so at least everything wasn't hanging out.

There was a nurse at a desk very near to my bed and the first thing that I did was to shout over.

"I want my clothes I want to get out of here"

The nurse looked over and told me I had to see the psychiatrist before anything would be decided. I could not be bothered with all of this and hollered back that I needed a drink and wanted to get to the pub and see my mates.

A doctor in a white coat came in and managed to sit me back down on the edge of my bed.

I was given a letter in a brown envelope and the doctor advised against me discharging myself. I had made my mind up and totally avoided the real issue; I had taken an overdose the night before and the pub was more important to me.

I managed to get my clothes and valuables back and within minutes I was heading out of the exit and on my way back to Teddington.

I went straight back to all my chaotic drinking buddies and they were concerned about me at first. After a few cans of our favourite; the events of the previous evening were soon forgotten.

It was summer time and the weather was scorching, we went to the big beer garden at the Anglers pub at Teddington Lock by the river Thames. It didn't take long to disturb the peace of civilized people drinking quietly in such beautiful surroundings.

I never really stopped to think how I affected other people, and I was with the right crowd so we all blended in together.

I did go back to the hostel that night and the staff didn't seem too phased about what had happened.

One of the girls who were staying there asked me to go to her room for a chat. She was genuinely concerned about my attempted suicide. She told me that when I went upstairs I had told Les I was taking all the sleepers and when Les later saw me in a coma state he came running down to tell staff.

At first the fellas on duty did not believe Les and they just palmed him off as though he was making up some cock and bull story.

After at least an hour or two when Les started screaming at them to call an ambulance; only then did they take action.

The paramedics had to take me down a few flights of narrow stairs strapped to a stretcher; not an easy task.

Les had probably saved my life; I would never forget that.

After that whole shenanigan I did not feel right about staying at the hostel.

I stayed another couple of nights and after a chat with my key-worker I said I was going it alone on the streets. He asked me had I any follow up from the hospital; I had lost the letter was given so I did not know or even care.

I later found out that the letter contained a follow up appointment with the local mental health service and was very important. Obviously I did not attend.

I found myself literally roaming the riverside in

Richmond; I even bumped into an old school mate and he went and nicked a couple of bottles of spirits from Sainsbury's. We got absolutely hammered in the sun and must have looked and sounded like a couple of down and outs. Anyway was that not what I had become!?

That first night I headed over to the parole hostel where Martin was living; he let me stay there a couple of nights before he was warned by the manager he would be evicted if he continued to let me stay. So that was out of the window and I continued to spend the days down at the river.

Richmond is one of the wealthiest areas in London and here I was homeless with only a few quid and literally falling apart.

At least there was a little crew of us who spent our days down there and we always came up with enough booze to see us through.

One lad who came down by the river was Lori. Out of all of us he seemed the most together and sensible. He never really drank as much as us and he had a great looking English Bull Terrier. He was also in great shape and looked like he worked out.

Lori kindly let me stay at his flat in Mortlake for a

few nights. He had a makeshift gym in the garden of his ground floor flat. Lori also had a tough old life and he had been housed by a housing association.

Lori loved kick boxing; he had a huge heavy punch bag hanging in his yard also.

It was like Lori genuinely wanted to help me; he got me on the weights and we even had a spar with gloves on. Even though I was always topping up on the Stella Lori got me out running through Richmond Park.

Lori could see that the booze was ruining me, and that considering I was a mess I was strong enough to work out and run. That kind of gave me a bit of hope which I held onto.

We were out on one of the afternoons in a little park near Mortlake brewery. A girl in her early twenties ran over to us; she loved Lori's dog. I got chatting to her and she even joined me on the drink. Bless her, she seemed like a damaged individual and maybe that is why we clicked at the time.

When I told her I was homeless she said there was an empty flat under her own home. She lived with her father and brother and her Dad owned both flats.

I spent the rest of the day with her and she took me downstairs to the flat which was derelict. It was so derelict that there were hardly any floorboards left or not even any running water. All I had was a sports bag with some clothes, a mobile phone a bit of cash and a toothbrush and toothpaste. Right there that was my world, I was not sure if I could get any lower. My new girlfriend said we had to keep quiet as her Dad would not be happy that I was squatting downstairs. We did end up having sex and she left me to crash on the floor that was left and got me a duvet to sleep under. Luckily it wasn't winter or I would have frozen. God knows how all those hardcore street people were able to survive like this.

Before I eventually got off to sleep I rang my sister and literally begged could I come and stay with her.

My sis had split up with her hubby so at least that made it a bit easier for her to agree that I could come down.

I had enough money for a coach to Ringwood where she picked me up. We never really spoke about that horrific night when I ruined her party and scared the life out of her kids. I just kept on drinking and I had never felt this close from breaking down in my life.

On the second day my Sis was meeting up with a load of friends and going to the beach at Durley Chine, Bournemouth. There was a big pub right by the beach but I didn't have enough to afford the coast of buying pints all day. I took a load of cans of Stella from the off license.

Again it was a red hot day and the beach was totally rammed. Sis and all her pals were having a great time and all in summer swimwear and shorts. I still had on my stinking jeans and generally felt like shite. I also felt so self conscious of the state I was in and could not snap out of it. I crashed face down in the sand for about an hour and when I woke I was aware of the buzz of happy people all around me.

I got so paranoid about the whole situation that I staggered over to the group that Sis was with and began an onslaught of abuse at her.

I screamed at sis to take me back to London that she did not give a shit about me; no one did! My thinking was by now well distorted. Again I was making a scene and embarrassing and hurting my sibling to the point that she was petrified. As she drove me back to Ringwood to get a coach she was sobbing all the way and all I could do carry on bellowing that no one gave a fuck about me.

At this rate it would be fair to say that no one should care about me. What had I become? An angry lunatic feeling mightily sorry for myself.

When I got back to London I had nowhere to go to. "Nowhere to run to, nowhere to hide" those famous lyrics were where I was at right now.

I phoned Joe, he had recently moved into a flat with Tiz up at Hanworth. I was lucky that they let me stay given my recent track record of chaos.

I slept on the floor of Joe's room, and I went window cleaning with him during the day.

I still kept in contact with SPEAR and continued to attend weekly meetings with Andy about my substance use.

I could not stay with Joe for long and he found an old camper van that belonged to a mate of ours Jamie.

The van was previously used to carry paint and tools as Jamie was a decorator just like me. But the van had now run its course and was fit for the scrap yard. It even had a puncture. We managed to tow my new home to a car park in Hampton Wick.

This must have been the only free car park for miles so we took advantage of that situation.

I had a duvet, pillows, some clothing and toiletries; that was all I needed. I had to go to the local petrol garage in the morning to use their toilet and washbasin.

I went to the gym in Teddington Pool so I could use the shower there to stop myself from stinking.

I told SPEAR about the van and they sent out an outreach guy every now and then in the middle of the night to verify I was staying there.

I was drinking cheap white cider at night to help me sleep and the van must have smelled rotten. But his was literally my life right now.

Most of my mates and girlfriends wanted me to keep away from them as I was having angry outbursts and behaving like a loon in public. This was how my mum was when I was a kid and I was turning into the character that I hated so much and was petrified of.

I lived in that van for around two months and it was

nearing the end of the summer and the nights were getting colder.

Then miraculously SPEAR had found a council flat for me run by Richmond Housing Partnership.

I met with them and completed all the formalities and was given a date to move in.

I still saw the mad Scotsman Les in Richmond and I told him my good news. I also gave him the keys of the camper van so he could take residence there.

Bless Les and all his bad luck because the day after he moved his belongings into the van new parking bays were marked out for metered parking.

The van was towed away by the council and Les had a nightmare trying to retrieve his bits and pieces which included his passport; his only valuable in the world.

When I was seeing Andy I spoke of how if I was ever to get my own place; that would be the answer to all my drinking problems.

I kidded myself that I would be able to control my alcohol use to a few cans every other day. I was wrong.

It all started well enough but soon I was going back

over to Teddington to be with the crazy crew.

I was now taking MDMA powder and was right back where I was when I first left Jan. I got complacent; I now had a decent flat to live in but it counted for nothing.

I got involved in other people's fights putting my neck on the line and started upsetting people who I never had a problem with before.

I got involved with a woman who lived over the road from me; she was on the crack-pipe and had a couple of sons from a traveller fella. My flat was in Hampton right opposite a traveller site that had been there for years.

I had knocked about with a gypsy family when I was younger so I had no bother with them at all.

The woman I was seeing had a lodger who was using heroin. She told me that he was leaving used foil and other bits in the toilet and her kids were finding it. The lad also had stopped paying his rent and was being a pain in the arse.

I asked if she wanted me to get rid of her nightmare tenant; and she was delighted at my offering of help. Why she had not asked the traveller boys to get rid of him I do not know. Maybe it was a case of being too proud.

This actually came back to save my skin about a month later. A good mate of mine I won't mention any names here came round fuming to my flat.

He told me that a lad we knew had hit his female cousin that day. I had always helped out before when it came to trouble and to be fair my pal had helped me. It was sort of a case of loyalty and just wanting to get involved in a fight for the sake of it.

The fella in question only lived over the road from me; right next to the traveller site. His other half was from gypsy origin as well from a well known family. I knew the boy well and never had any bother with him before but my mind was screwed up so I agreed to go over and put the frighteners on him.

My pal did say he only wanted me to scare him, but I went a little bit over the top. I took a big kitchen knife with me just for effect.

As usual I had already been drinking loads and was well fuelled up. We drove over and parked the motor away round the corner.

I went straight over to the back wall of the house where the lad was living. My mate held back and his behind a wall so as not to be seen.

I screamed up at the window for the offender to come outside. At first he didn't want to know but when I entered into the back garden he came legging it downstairs and straight out into the back yard.

For some reason I pulled out the knife but was never going to use it.

"You going to stab me you cunt?" he screamed at me

"I don't need to you mug" was my defiant reply.

I then put the blade back in my back pocket and he ran back indoors. All of a sudden his partner whose house it was charged out and punched me on the side of my nose. I was aware that she was wearing a chunky gold sovereign ring and that connected and cut my nose.

I taunted her;

"Is that the best shot you've got!?" she then bolted out the back gate and ran off down toward the travellers site.

Then the mush came back with what looked like a single bore shotgun in his hands.

"I'll fuckin shoot ya!" he raged at me

"Go on then do it!" I smirked back. And to be honest right then it would not have bothered me if he did.

Just like when I had swallowed all those sleepers at the hostel I had not care or regard for me my life right now.

My reply stunned him and he relaxed his grip on the gun.

There was still no sign of my pal who I came to help in the first place; he was still out of sight.

I decide it was time to go; I had done more enough for something that did not concern me.

I then saw a load of the traveller lads grouped up over by the dark alleyway that connected their site.

I was expecting them to charge over and do me with golf clubs or other tools. For some reason they walked back down the narrow walkway and out of sight.

I walked back to the car and my mate was already sitting back in the driver's seat.

"I only asked to shout up at the window and scare

the fucker!"

I replied that I had lost it and just saw red and went for it. God knows what shit I had started now.

My good friend explained to me that the lads other half had gone and got the traveller boys and when they came back they recognized me.

"That's Dave he is ok leave him" one of them had ordered.

My pal had heard them and thought I was in big trouble and yet I was let off with no trouble.

I later found out that one of the sons of the woman who I had helped out with getting rid of her lodger was among them.

That had saved me from a certain reprisal from the lads on the site.

After this incident there was a rumour going round that I had stabbed the lad in the foot; which was nonsense.

I was actually gutted I had got myself involved this time; as I had never had an issue with the lad across the road and I had always liked him.

This was just another incident to make me more

paranoid and make me feel even lesser than I did about myself.

The year was now 2004 and my football banning order was at an end. It had been six years since I had been able to watch QPR in a live match.

It was pre-season and we were going to play Ajax of Amsterdam at home. Ajax are well know for their hooligan element and this would be a lively game with an intense atmosphere.

I was really looking forward to catching up with all the chaps again and finally going in to see my team play at the blue pearl in the oyster of West London; Loftus Road!

The arrangement was to meet up in the West End and have a few pints there before heading back to the Bush for more pre-match drinks.

I headed up West and we met in a pub around Leicester Square somewhere. There was around twenty of us and all good lads from back in the day and still regular attendees of the matches.

Usually I would have been in good spirits and having a good laugh and joke. But I had changed and was on edge and self-conscious of the state I was in. All the shit I was taking and too much booze had taken its toll on me.

Instead of the usual camaraderie it was as though I had to prove a point to save my own pride.

I acted like a complete nutter all afternoon and when one of the lads Roy told me to calm it down I turned on him.

I was so full of rage, paranoia and frustration that I was taking it out on my own band of brothers.

It was only that the lads could see I was in a downward spiral that I got away with being such a prick.

I showed up another of my best mates Neil by offering people out on the underground train on the way back to Shepherds Bush. The other boys had disowned me by now.

Somehow we managed to get back to the Springbok which was the pub right by the ground without me getting a good slap or being nicked.

Well I had made it back to the home of QPR; but not for long!

Just before kick off we headed toward the ground and across the road was a group of Ajax fans singing and being loud.

I just ran over to them and confronted them all.

I shouted at them "Come on you Ajax cunts!" I just wanted a fight at any cost.

The old bill came over and warned me to get away and he even asked Neil to get me to the game and away from trouble.

As usual I did not listen and I ran back over in an attempt to get at the Ajax boys.

That was enough for me to be nicked and cuffed. So there you go I did not make it back to watch the team I had supported since the age of eight years old.

To cut a long story short I appeared back at West London Magistrates and received another three year ban from football. This was my fourth banning order a total of eleven years and would be nine consecutive years without ever going to a game.

This was also the first time I had signed on for benefits since I left school; I wasn't even mentally fit for work even though I wanted to.

I was in such a state now that I could not leave my flat in the morning to go to the shop about a hundred yards away. I had heard about recluses who left their curtains pulled shut. Well I could not face letting in any daylight until I had a few cans of lager.

I had to phone over to my lady friend across the street and ask her to go and get four cans for me before I could start going out into the world again.

I was not physically dependant on alcohol; it was more of a psychological thing for me. Although it wouldn't have taken much longer before the shakes and seizures got hold of me. I had stopped eating regularly and my kitchen cupboards and fridge were bare.

Having to live in a filthy old van was a low point in my life; but my mental state now was even lower.

Mikey came over every now and then and he asked me to go and see his Nan in hospital as she was dying.

Peggy had been a very close person in my life; back when I was living with Mikey I was at Peggy's every day to walk the dogs and have lunch and tea.

She was a salt of the earth and absolute diamond with one of the kindest souls of anyone I had ever met. I went to see her with Mikey and had a laugh with her; that was last time I saw Peggy; she died not long after.

Mikey was gutted and so was I, of course I was going to attend her funeral.

I was still going round the mad house in Teddington with the other drinking crew. The night before the funeral I stayed there as it was nearer the cemetery and chapel where the service was going to be held.

I woke up late and I was in a real mess; I had to get to the shop to get a couple of cans to face it all. I missed the departure time to go with the cars following the hearse. I rang Mikey and he said to pick up the procession as it went past the police station in Teddington.

I swigged back a can to steady myself and ran down Broad Street and met the cars as they drove slowly down toward the bridge. What a state I must have looked; I borrowed a suit from one of the lads and it didn't fit too well!

There was a very big turnout for Peggy as she was a very popular lady.

During the service I lost control and sobbed like a baby; I showed myself right up.

After the service we went briefly back to Mikey's

mums house and then round the corner to the Clarence pub where the wake was being held.

The Clarence is a big pub and back in the 80's had a small nightclub which was now a restaurant. It was our old hunting ground the scene of many a mad night and fights with the bouncers. This was 2004 and most of us were settling down with kids and good jobs; well I wasn't and it showed.

I was OK for a while in the pub talking to the family and old friends but I soon got worse for wear again.

Mikey's cousin Graham told me straight I had to shape up and sort myself out. I didn't want to hear this I took that as an insult. It dented my pride; instead of taking that on the chin I reacted in a bad way.

I began ranting and raving at Graham and stormed out the big double doors into the entrance outside. As I stopped outside I looked back in through the big windows and crashed my elbow through the glass.

The tall window shattered all over the ground and luckily I had not hurt myself. Mikey came running out and insisted I apologize to everyone and to the landlord. I told him to fuck off and stormed off down the road.

Mikey grabbed my arm and made me go back and sit outside the pub. He told me that the old bill had been called and it would be better if I just waited for them to arrive.

When the police van arrived instead of apologizing to them and the governor I just carried on ranting on and shouting.

So I was nicked and taken to my favourite place Twickenham Police Station.

I don't remember much about the journey or the procedure at the sergeant's desk. I must have crashed as soon as I hit the blue mattress in my cell.

13. SEEING THE LIGHT

I awoke with a blinding light in my eyes and I could see Peggy's face looking down on me.

I could hear her voice telling me I had to stop doing what I was doing. Peggy was the only person I was going to listen to; although she was gone, I believe she was there looking down on me. I saw the light literally and when I heard Peggy telling me off that was enough for me.

I had not even been able to act like an adult for that one day, I was a disgrace.

How many more times did I need to hit rock bottom? How lower could I go?

Now was the time to stop this shit; I had been too long in contemplation now was time for some action.

Luckily I was released without charge; either the landlord felt sorry for which I doubt or the family had a word with him not to press charges.

It was time to get real, to wake up and start dealing with the main issue and that was to stop drinking alcohol.

It was now clear that alcohol did not agree with me; I now had twenty eight convictions. I had been to prison five times, received four football banning orders and nearly lost my life on many occasions.

It had taken me all the way to nearly losing my marbles; I was an angry paranoid wreck.

I phoned Andy my alcohol counsellor and told him about my latest arrest. He had heard and seen it all before; but this time I made a pledge to stop drinking from this very day October 4th 2004.

I know I had blown out the residential rehab and had said that getting housed would sort out my issue. I could see now that I had been kidding myself and I said to Andy I would now do whatever it took to keep off the demon drink.

Andy asked me to come to Richmond to see him for any immediate support that was needed.

I did not to go in for an inpatient detoxification; I had stopped before for the two weeks and for the two months when I was still with Jan.

Sleeping tablets were a bit of a sore subject after my overdose at the hostel so I got prescribed some meds just to take the edge away.

Andy made loads of calls and got me a referral to a Structured Day Programme in Hounslow. I would have to go there the next day for an assessment and take a look at the place.

I was nervous and anxious as hell; apart from the time I went up to see the rehab in Reading I had not ever made a commitment of this scale.

The centre was called EACH and was in the heart of Hounslow right at the beginning of the High Street. I sheepishly walked in and there was a young Indian lady, quite attractive and had a lovely smile on her face.

She made me feel welcome and I sat on a seat by the window wondering what this was going to be about.

It seemed like I was waiting there for ages and I could easily have just walked out and never came back. But if I did run away would I ever face my demons again?

When I made my decision I was at what is called the jumping off point. I was ready to jump off a cliff and by staying in this waiting area I was now going to jump off the crazy merry go round that was my life of chaos.

A young Indian fella came out with a clip-board in his hands; he called my name and I sat up and said "Yeh that's me".

I got up and followed the man into a small cubicle like room along the corridor. I could see that there were two other rooms like this and a bigger room off to the left; the door was closed and I could a group of people in there.

This fella looked quite serious but welcoming at the same time; he introduced himself as Avtar and said he was the head counsellor and lead of the day programme.

Avtar was going to carry out an assessment to see if I was suitable to attend the program which would last for twelve weeks and include weekly one to one counselling sessions.

One of the questions was about my history of drug and alcohol use.

I told Avtar how it had all started right back to my glue sniffing days and right up to my recent incident at Peggy's wake at the Clarence.

I could tell Avtar had been there himself; he jokingly said that I had now had my fair share of booze and other substances and surely I had had enough now.

He was spot on; I was beaten from it all but it was all very scary to me how would I face a life without the booze.

The Structure Day Programme would teach me a new way of looking at things. The more honest I was with my self and others would have a better grounding for a good recovery from all the madness throughout my life.

I agreed that I would abide by group rules and signed the form to sign up for the SDP. Avtar was already aware that Andy had been granted funding for my place on this SDP.

I was going to start the following Monday and would attend every day Monday to Friday. In a way it was like a rehab centre only I would be going home each afternoon.

I managed to stay sober over the weekend and in a way I was actually looking forward to getting stuck in to whatever was going to come up on the SDP.

I had never done anything like this before; I certainly was not scared of being in a group. All the years I had gone to football and the pub and club scene was about being around others. I had never been a lone drinker except for the last days of my drinking when I could not face going out without first having those couple of cans.

I got a number 111 bus from the bottom of my road all the way to literally opposite EACH in Hounslow; that sure made life easier for me.

The reception area was starting to get busy and there were people there I would not have expected to have problems with alcohol. There were a lot of Asians and English attending; mainly older than myself and there were a couple of lads and women around my age.

Every morning we all would be in the group sitting in a circle around the room. The facilitator would ask each one of us to "check-in" a chance to say how we were feeling and what was going on for each of us.

Some of the group members did not want to say much and just said they were "fine" or OK.

As I listened to some of the others open up and be totally honest with us and them I could see it was OK to say how I really was feeling.

I had never been able to express myself before, my mother or father had never asked how I was. All I knew was to show anger to ward people off and if I was feeling fearful or anxious I would never admit that to anyone.

There were different facilitators each day and they taught us different ways of looking at our past and our present wellbeing.

Some of it was a bit too deep and confusing for me so I started to take the good stuff that I related to on board.

The group was very diverse and so the dynamics were very therapeutic. I did not realize that at the time how certain people or situations could make me react in a certain way.

On a Friday morning the group was "open" to previous members and other people who just wanted that bit of support once a week.

There were a few people on the open group that had been to residential rehab and sounded like they were in good form.

Then on a Friday afternoon we had a facilitator called Finbar and old Irishman than seemed so calm and peaceful. He openly told us that he had attended Alcoholics Anonymous for many years and still did so.

Finbar started to teach us about Step One, the first part of the 12 steps of AA.

Step one was about admitting I was an alcoholic and that my life had become unmanageable while I was drinking. That was so right; my life was in tatters before I came into this day programme. I wasn't working any more, and I was physically going down hill. My mental state was terrible too; all the anxiety, guilt, anger and depression had led me here.

One of the group rules and something I had to agree to and sign on the dotted line was to remain sober and abstinent from any other substance.

I was doing well I had not drank or taken anything since that morning I woke in the police cell after Peggy's wake.

Finbar would ask if anyone had or felt like drinking. If anyone was sounding like they were going to drink he would just say "go to a meeting".

Finbar kept drumming it in to us to attend an AA meeting as often as possible.

It took me a few weeks to muster up the courage to go to an AA meeting. And thankfully I was not going to go on my own; I went with another fella on the group.

I can remember it so well; the meeting was in a small community hall in Hounslow on the same road as the police station.

We arrived slightly early and as I walked round to the entrance of the building there was a few people standing outside; some smoking. The levels of anxiety inside of me were immense.

I had never felt so self conscious in my life; I had stood before judges waiting to be sentenced. I had run into big mobs of rival fans at football; I had climbed through windows of shops to rob them. Yet here I was among other down to earth people with the same problem as me and I could not look them in the eye.

When I saw someone who was sober and seemed so content I just could not understand how they could be so calm and happy.

I was still in very early days of being sober and my

mentality for all those years was how I could ever get through a day without alcohol.

Everyone was so welcoming except those who were probably feeling the same as me.

I kept my head down and listened to the person sharing their experience and hope. But to be honest I was so messed up I could hardly take anything in.

It was suggested to keep coming back and just get my bum on the seat; that was a winner to start with.

Back at the day programme at EACH, I was getting on with it well and actually started to enjoy what I was learning.

My anger started to seep out in the groups and in my one to one counselling.

Toward the end of the first twelve week program it was suggested that I attend a Personal Development course at Richmond adult college. This was like a follow on and starting to get a bit deeper.

The course was run by qualified psychotherapists and was based on a theory called Transactional Analysis. Basically every person is always in a psychological made; Parent, Adult or Child.

I was taught that the way we interact with others depends on what mode we are in.

One of the first exercises we had to do in the course was to draw on a large bit of flip chart paper. We had to create an image of our family all together in a snap shot.

I looked at the others while they were drawing; some of the people on the course wore suits straight from work and there were not many others there that I thought I would relate to.

There was another young woman who joined this course; Lauretta and she was from Hounslow West and was the only one I thought had a similar upbringing to me.

Everyone except for me drew their family. We all had to talk about our picture and as we went round the room I was so full of myself I hardly listened to the others. In my head I wanted to explode and waited for my turn so I could unleash my rage toward my family.

When the facilitators asked me to talk about my snap shot I just flipped.

"I can't draw anything; my family is fucked I have no family!" I bellowed through the room.

I was encouraged to explain further and that it was OK to be angry.

It was after the class had finished that I could see the therapeutic value behind the exercise.

The following week we were asked to write a life history; as long as it needed to be.

This time I did start listening to the others and what I heard was tragic stories just like my own. This was a turning point for me to realize that I was not the only one that had a broken home and family.

The guy who wore the immaculate suit and had a great job with a big salary up in London also had a horrible upbringing.

My problem had been a hatred of the world; that I was inferior and everyone else had a perfect life with "normal" families.

At least I now knew that most people have a sad tale to tell; this eased my rage and anger and self pity.

I listened intently to the others and I actually felt a close connection with them for the first time in my life.

There was another fella there who said he had started his life story but could not finish it. The following week he was not present at the group. We were told that sadly he had taken his own life that week.

This really was a very deep and delving look into our own lives and if someone was not ready to look inwards that could be fatal as this proved to be.

At EACH I learned the consequences of my years of drinking and substance abuse. We did an exercise to calculate how much I had spent on the booze over the years. This was to include court fines, loss of earnings due to being locked up and the actual cost of alcohol and other drugs.

I was mortified when I totaled it all up to be well over £150.000. I could have had a new car; paid for the flat I had with Jan and lived a very comfortable life.

Add to the monetary cost the effect on my physical and mental wellbeing it was a disaster of monumental proportions.

Other costs were that I had never been on holiday with my mates; I had not watched QPR for what would have been nine years when my ban ended in 2007. It was still 2005 now.

QPR had been relegated to the old 2nd Division which is now League 1. We had been in a play off final with Cardiff and also been promoted by winning the division away at Sheffield Wednesday where around 10.000 R's fans had turned out.

I gave up my marriage and my mortgage and was now banned from driving; the list went on and on.

I learned that I had not grown up that I was still mentally at the age when I starting to use glue to shut out all my emotions and it was an escape from the horrors of my mothers' anger and drinking. So I was kind of stuck as a thirteen year old inside a thirty seven year old body.

And when I looked at it; that was how I had been acting as a teenager screaming out to be heard; but did not know how to in an adult fashion.

This was my chance to re-learn and grow back into an adult again. This was going to be a lifetime's process and still is to this day.

At AA I heard a saying; it's about "Progress not perfection". I had to get my head round that one as I thought everyone else expected me to be perfect and that led to guilt and self consciousness on a high level.

I started to realize that nobody did expect me to be perfect it was in my own head and that led to resentment toward others.

That first year of me being sober was very hard mentally; I had so much shit inside my head that it needed sorting.

I was told it was like deleting old files from a computer and installing a new cleaner software.

At EACH we were encouraged to not get into a relationship and focus on ourselves. Myself and Lauretta who I met at personal development started dating; I had no intentions of getting in a relationship but it just started to happen.

We really encouraged each other throughout the course and felt very close straight away.

I got a sponsor at AA and started to work through the 12 steps. I still was finding it hard to be myself and totally honest about my feelings and was still full of anxiety at the meetings.

My fist sober Christmas was the year before and I had only stopped drinking for two months. I had my mum over to stay and it was a disaster; we did not get on at all. My counsellor at EACH said it had all been too much too soon; but I felt I had to make up with mum. It did not work.

My second Christmas and I was with Lauretta and she asked me to come for Christmas lunch with her family to a pub in Greenford.

I did not feel I was ready to be able to cope with all the drinking and Lauretta's mum's partner was a big drinker.

I made it through the lunch OK although it was hard seeing everyone demolish all that booze. Then we were to go to a party at one of their friends. Back there the booze flowed and I white knuckled the ride; it was very uncomfortable.

Somehow I got through the evening without drinking and got back home safely.

Lauretta's birthday is 28th December and we ended up having a bit of an argument. This triggered me into buying four cans of Stella.

Another very pertinent saying I had heard during all the groups was what goes through someone's mind when they are about to relapse.

There is always a build up to relapse without the person really being aware of that. And the final event or situation that is the greatest excuse to pick up the can or glass is the straw that broke the camels back.

My final straw was this row with Lauretta and the last two words that go through the mind is "Fuck it!"

Although I purchased the four cans I did not actually drink them. I had them in my fridge for two days. I believe I was trying to test myself to the limit to see if I could leave them.

I took the cans down to the bins at my flat and left them by the bin shed door. This was Christmas present for the bin men!

News Years Eve was fast approaching and that is another trigger for any alcoholic or addict in early recovery.

The famous two words popped up like a window on my laptop; "Fuck it!" I phoned Mart my best pal and told him I was going to drink again.

I got myself a whole crate of Kronenbourg as the shop did not have Stella and spent the evening round Mart's on Butts Farm. I sat there can in hand for the whole night except when we went briefly next door to see people I had not seem for a while.

Word had got out that I was round and some lads I had trouble with previously were circling round like vultures waiting for something to happen.

All that happened was me waking up on Mart's sofa the next morning; there was a pool of puke on the floor and I felt like absolute shit. This was the hangover of all hangovers. Had I really enjoyed the evening? It was good to be back socializing again but as for the booze then no I had not.

I rang Lauretta and I feared that we would be finished so I convinced her that I could control my drinking again.

I would only have a couple of bottles every other day and still attend the Personal Development course.

I had also learned that addiction is an obsession of the mind. Once I had taken that first drink again all my thinking was around my next drink. Although I had convinced myself I could take it or leave it that was nonsense.

The days I was not drinking I would be planning ahead to the next big one and that would be on

Friday.

Friday came and again I bought another crate. This time I felt even worse and I was about to lose Lauretta as well.

14. RECOVERY

That Friday night I had a dream and it felt so real almost as if it really was happening.

I dreamt that a priest was before me with a huge crucifix; he was holding the cross with both hands. The father dressed in his black robe and dog collar pressed the cross to my forehead and I felt it burning into me.

"Demons be gone forever" the vicar shouted into me and it was like a load of evil spirits had been sucked out of my body.

I awake with the feeling that I was cleansed and I made a decision again there and then never to drink again.

I rang a fella I knew at AA and asked him to sponsor me and take me through the 12 steps again. I told him I had just had a bit of a lapse again and about the dream.

I asked Dave my new sponsor to kick my arse and get strict with me. I had to ring him every morning and meet up at least once a week to go through the steps.

Dave had a Boxer dog and we met up in Bushy Park Teddington my old haunting grounds as a kid.

It all felt very spiritual and calming sitting there by the old boating pond and I started to get honest again.

I got back to Step Four in good time as that was not a problem I wanted sobriety so badly this time; no messing around with it.

I had heard the expression that when someone relapses they go out to do some research. I certainly had researched into myself and finally admitted I could not control my drinking. It was as if I had to prove to myself that I could not control it to actually make that final admittance and decision.

Step Four is about making a fearless and honest inventory about ourselves and to see my part in situations and events.

This opened me up into a whole new way of

perceiving events and how I had affected other people with my actions.

I wrote well over a thousand items and felt like I had covered everything.

It was all about being willing to change my old ways and start making amends to everyone or thing that I had hurt.

Dave explained that not everyone would accept my apology or that some would not even see that I had done any wrong in the first place. It was more about making myself feel clear of my conscience and that at least I had tried to make amends.

This process was a very enlightening experience it had lifted a lot of my guilt and made me feel a lot better about myself. Now it was about continuing to see the error of my ways and acting accordingly whenever I did feel I had acted a bit off.

Again it was about progress not perfection and to not beat myself up for any wrong doings.

When I say wrong doings I mean the way I think about someone or their actions and how I react to or perceive an event or situation. This stops any resentment which can ultimately lead to bad feelings again.

So I continued to attend regular AA meetings and also completed a second SDP and Personal Development course. After my lapse I was now right back on course.

Lauretta supported me. We were soul mates from the very beginning.

All the counselling and groups were helping me to start transforming into the person I was meant to be.

This was the longest I had ever been out of work; but I was working on myself to start becoming an adult again.

It was suggested to get into some voluntary work and attend further courses. I decided to learn counselling skills and also all about drugs and their different affects.

I had been a painter most of my life so far and now I wanted to be able to help others in the same boat as me.

For the first time in my life I started to listen and be wrapped up in my own world. The counselling skills helped me to become interested in other people and their problems.

I managed to get a voluntary position helping out at a drug and alcohol service in Southall.

This was right down in Old Southall and that area is full of illegal immigrants, sex workers and is overrun with heroin and crack dealers and users.

There is never a dull moment in places like that and there is always someone so much more worse off than myself.

I went through Level 2 Counselling and continued my voluntary work.

I now decided it was time to get back into some paid work and a job came up at the Salvation Army hostel in Hammersmith. The hostel was further up by Olympia an area I loved from my days at QPR.

I had also moved out my flat and did an exchange with a young woman who had a one bed flat in Chiswick.

I could not believe my luck that someone would want to move away from Chiswick. Bless her she had some problems and I think she had upset everyone in the block and needed to get away.

The flat was in a right state and a few others had turned it down. This was meant to be for me; so I applied my decorating skills and made it look decent.

Chiswick is only a few miles from QPR and I would be allowed back in about a year's time and I was near to my new employment in Hammersmith.

Everything started to fit in and life was looking a lot better. I remained sober and kept out of any bother.

The biggest reason I moved away from Hanworth was to get away from my old life. I had caused a lot of trouble there and no offense to all my mates but they were all still drinking and using coke.

Moving away made it easier for me to move forward; I was not running away but just needed to be out of the equation.

I worked two night shifts in the hostel and another evening at the centre in Southall.

I also carried on attending AA meetings and funnily enough the hostel even had a meeting held there each week.

It had not been so long ago that I was in the same shoes as the lads in this hostel and there were some right characters in there.

Some of the staff was so judgemental toward the drinkers and addicts in the hostel but I had to bite my tongue and keep quiet. Had I have been a lot more further down the line in my own recovery I would have felt more confident to challenge them on this.

Addiction is a crazy thing you can offer support and point people in the right direction but it almost is always a losing battle. That is the nature of the beast and I was taught that you just have to let people do what they need to do.

I now had started to attend Level 3 counselling and this was more about the different theories.

I started to learn about Freud and Carl Jung and their theory. It is so interesting and really began to learn so much more about myself and others behaviours.

Even if I was to never become a counsellor myself this would be put me in great stead to get along with the rest of the world and other people.

I started to become aware of why I acted the way I did; where my anger was coming from. I had to attend counselling sessions myself as part of the learning and I started to get even deeper and gradually rid myself of all the old hurt and unhelpful behaviours.

I passed Level 3 with flying colours and decide to go the whole way and attend the two year Diploma course. If I was successful this would mean that I would be a qualified counsellor myself.

I had to find a placement with a counselling service and complete 100 hours of voluntary counselling of others.

Luckily I was able to start doing my hours at Southall in the drug service I was already volunteering at.

I left the hostel and now took the leap back into full time employment. I had been putting business cards through doors all round Hammersmith and Chiswick. I was ready to go back painting and decorating and my I got a few calls from my cards.

I got a call from a plumber/ builder who lived just off Kings Street in Hammersmith. I went to the fella's house to meet him and he was the campest Gay fella which I found very amusing.

He had a partner as well and they both looked like they were very successful and their home was immaculate.

I was offered loads of work and started to earn good money again.

There were a couple of lads working for them who were right on the coke and as I was further down the line in my own recovery I was OK with this. I just focused on my work but I let them know that I did not drink or take anything anymore. They were good lads and respected this; all I did not need was for someone to keep offering me stuff or to encourage me to go drinking.

Lauretta was living with me now and she had got herself a job at a golf course in Chiswick. Lauretta worked behind the bar and fair play to her that was something I would not feel too comfortable with.

We were both in the middle of studying the Diploma in counselling and we were both able to help each other.

I had now managed to get a full time job working at the drug service in Southall and the salary was very decent.

I had my first counselling client who was a young lad who had got into a lot of trouble with the law. He was a heavy skunk smoker and all I could really try and do was help him with his cravings and how to mange them.

I was still managing my own cravings for alcohol as an ongoing process. What I had now learned was that it was not really a "craving" as such but more a mere thought.

It was all about the thinking and what I was telling myself in my own head.

I could help others realize this; but if someone does not want to make changes it is a very tough task.

There is an old saying; you can lead the horse to the water but you cannot make it drink.

I did loads of training at CRI the company I worked for and was always updating and completing courses.

Over the years I successfully passed an Open University qualification for drug and alcohol professionals.

I also passed my Diploma for counselling; I was now qualified.

I did various roles within CRI; I assessed problematic alcohol users at Ealing Hospital and even went once a week to GP surgeries in the Ealing borough to provide brief interventions for patients referred by their doctor.

The year there was an outbreak of Swine Flu; I became ill and had to isolate in my bed for a week. In that week I developed a relapse prevention program for offenders who had been arrested and tested positive for Class A substances such as Heroin, Crack and powder cocaine.

I loved it; I could empathize with these people and I believe they knew that I knew!

I Love that old saying "If you know you know"!

I was earning good money and only worked Monday to Friday but new protocols came into force. The government and funders wanted us all to keep a lot of paperwork and record evidence of progress made with our service users.

It became a tick box and recording exercise more than the actual face to face work and personal touch that was needed by these vulnerable people.

When I used to see Andy in Richmond; he stuck with me and there never seemed any rush for me to sort myself out.

It was as though we had to now almost tell people to hurry up and sort out their ingrained alcohol and drug addictions. It really does not work like that. I had never in my life before earned good money like this week in and week out.

I had always been self-employed and in and out of painting jobs.

So I started to save a few quid; Lauretta was working as well so we decided to go on our first holiday abroad.

We were now a good few years sober and felt confident enough to go on an All Inclusive holiday.

When we were first in recovery we had to be very careful not to get into situations that could trigger alcohol use.

It takes time and a lot of work on myself to get to that stage where I knew inside myself I could deal with people drinking like crazy on holiday.

We ended up going to a hotel in Salou; which is just south of Barcelona. The hotel had three main buildings.

One was where all the English stayed and the other two seemed to be for all the other Europeans. It was as though us English were being kept away from the others!

In the evenings we could go to the other buildings for dinner and the food was top notch.

We enjoyed our holiday so much that we booked up for the following year. We met some lovely people there and hooked up with them again.

When we went back the next year there was a lad there who had been drinking all day; just like I used to. He was a big fella and was so pissed he had to be taken back up to his room. It took four other blokes to get him in the left and back up safely.

When we went home we were back in the airport and having a coffee and bite to eat in the canteen.

I saw the big lad and went over to say hello. I joked with him that it looked like he had a good time and mentioned the evening he had to be helped upstairs.

Then surprisingly he got a bit embarrassed and told me he had been sober for three years and had relapsed. He was honest enough to say he thought he was strong enough to come on this holiday what with all the free booze on flow!

He had been volunteering just like me in a drug service and this was a bit of a set-back.

This was another harsh reminder to me just how serious this old drinking lark can be.

My football ban had ended in 2007; which was well before this holiday. It had been another year since the relapse I had and I was feeling good to go back and not get in any aggro at the games.

When I first went back to QPR I got a half season ticket and sat on my own in the paddock; a small side seated area and right near the away fans!

I actually sat there without getting the hump with the opposition fans and I even stayed there for the whole ninety minutes without having to keep sneaking off to the bar!

QPR started to play well again and were pushing for promotion and I was really enjoying the matches. It took that half season for me to start meeting up with the lads again and go with them.

I was able to go in the pubs and not feel uncomfortable around all the drinking.

Neil Warnock became our manager and took us forward. We had players like Adel Taraabt, Routledge and staunch midfielder Shaun Derry and good old Clint Hill in defense.

There was one game though where I nearly lost it again.

We were playing Swansea at home and me and Mart met up with everyone at the Smuts pub by the White City estate. This had been a good meeting place for years; this particular game everyone was in there and was great to chat and see old mates again.

Now to be honest there was a load of Swansea fans around looking for trouble and it was kicking off before and after the match.

I got a bit excited again and really had to contain myself from getting in to another ruck.

The same thing over the past few years with Millwall, Cardiff, Leeds and all the other clubs that have a big hooligan following.

It is too easy to find myself in a situation and be arrested again, so now I just walk away or explain to my mates I do not want the aggro any more.

As I write this sentence it is 2020 and I have not been arrested or been to court since way back in 2004 the morning I woke up and heard good old Peggy telling me off in the police cell.

Jason who I lived with back in 1989 has written a book on how football violence is an addiction. I had spoken to him on the phone about that and totally agree that it is.

There is a definition of insanity: doing the same things over and over and expecting a different outcome. That really is addiction all over; whether it's a substance, food, sex, gaming or in this case football violence.

I do not know or cannot prove that everyone who gets involved in trouble at football has an addictive personality but it is like an extreme sport where the adrenaline rush is very strong.

I can analyze myself now and look back at why I did these things. It stems back to when I beat that lad who was bullying me. I received a lot of respect after that and felt it was the way to go.

Add to that I was already abusing substances so I was always looking for an escape and a high.

There is a sense of danger at football and for some that become addictive. It is a being part of pack or a surrogate family and feeling accepted and being "someone" that others look up to.

What I am trying to achieve is to be content with

myself and not feel the need to be "accepted" by others.

I had not played any sport for years and because I was not focused on just buying cans after work I got involved again.

I started a six-a-side football team with Mart's sons and my good mates Mick and Steve. I always was a good goalkeeper; we got in a league in Turnham Green, Chiswick and even won it a couple of times.

I started playing cricket again; I had not played since my school days. I became a member at Barnes CC and played regularly for the 4th team and the Sunday side.

And more recently I trained to do a white collar boxing event with Steve. I enjoyed the training; it kept me fit and following that I joined a boxing gym in Pokesdown in Bournemouth.

Myself and Lauretta decided to move to Bournemouth to be nearer my mate Mart and also my sister lived down there.

My mum had moved down here back in the late 90s but did not get on with my sis so was left a bit isolated.

My mum died just before I moved down; this sounds really bad but I was relived for mum as her life was awful. She still suffered from her mental health issues and had pushed everyone away from herself.

The day before my 51st birthday I had an unlicensed boxing bout and went the three rounds and just lost on points. It was close but was more about the fact I had done it.

If I had taken up boxing as a kid who knows? I just had not guidance so I went my own way in life and that was to fight on the streets.

If I had of carried on drinking I believe I would have been stabbed to death by now. The kids have no respect for anything any more. There is a big push for "knives down and gloves up!" boxing teaches respect and commitment.

A lot of the kids these days come from broken families and just like me have no role models or parents to point them in the right direction.

I must say that although I have a very broken family; Lauretta's mother has been brilliant she has never judged me for my past and has been there for us both. So I do now feel "accepted".

When I moved to Bournemouth we had a lot of trouble with neighbours; it was hell so we eventually got a transfer to a better block of flats.

I could walk to the beach in fifteen minutes and for the first time in my life I get a dog.

I never had kids so my dog who is a Jack Russell crossed with a Bichon Friese is like my son and best friend. It's true what they say; a dog is man's best friend loyal to the core.

I set up my own painting business in Bournemouth and started to get some good customers and did a lot of work for a top notch builder.

Lauretta was never really happy in Bournemouth it was really my decision to move from London.

After three years of being on the South Coast Lauretta decided she wanted to go back to where her father came from; Donegal in North West Ireland.

15. A NEW LIFE

My sister has never really forgiven me for the past; I can't really blame her.

I decided to change myself and forgive mum and also forgive myself.

Alcoholics Anonymous helped me to forgive and also make amends to those we had hurt.

Unfortunately not everyone will forgive and my sis is one of those. I love her but have to get on with my own life.

It was a very spontaneous decision to come to Ireland; it was done in a mad hurry.

Lauretta came over and got a job and decided to stay with her Aunt. They then found a lovely bungalow to rent in the hills and very near to the bakery where she got a job.

I literally had to sell any furniture we had and give

up our council tenancy to follow Lauretta over to Ireland.

I now have a job in the same bakery; the money is poor but we are able to save as there are not so many outlays over here.

Back in England I could never seem to get anywhere always struggling to make ends meet. So I know I have made the right decision to start a new life again at the age of fifty three.

At the very beginning of this book I described of how the men in white coats came to take my mum away.

I was very nearly taken away too; I was one of the lucky ones who had a "divine intervention" moment.

I am not super religious but I believe I have been saved; I do not know why but I am still here to tell my tale.

I had many close encounters with death without realizing it.

My life was just the way it was; I do not set out to glorify any violent behaviour. I just did not know any better.

There are so many other events I could of written about and I have left out a lot of things I am not proud of and did not want to share.

I have left out some people's names as I do not want to embarrass you. If I have offended anyone I am sorry but it is what it is.

I still have very tough days where I find it difficult to be "happy". Life is hard but it is as hard as I choose it to be.

Since I got sober I've achieved so many things; I did not know how get through a day without drinking. I have been on all inclusive holidays; I lost my mum and went to her bedside in A and E and her hand was still warm to the touch. I did not drink.

I went to see QPR win at Wembley in the Play-off final; I did not drink.

I got married to Lauretta and did not drink at our wedding.

I have gone back to basics working in a bakery for minimum wage. Maybe it is better just to lead a simple life.

Here in Donegal there is no traffic, no speed humps, and no parking restrictions. I live in one of the most scenic and beautiful places in the world.

I am still working on myself to accept myself who I really am and to have a meaningful marriage to Lauretta.

At the age of fifty I took up boxing mainly to keep fit but also to prove to myself I could fight in a controlled manner.

I am a born survivor and will beat my demons. I believe I have beaten my addictions and have made a decision not to drink ever again. I know the AA theory is just one day at a time and it is good to live in the day.

I have also found out two things that I now find very important to myself staying sober. Firstly just before mum died I asked her which came first; her drinking or her mental health issues. Mum told me that her alcoholism had led to her being diagnosed as Bi-Polar with psychotic tendencies.

My Dad also opened up to me when I went over to see him in Australia. He admitted to me that when he had left mum there had been a huge fight. I was a little lad and started screaming and got in the way of them both. Dad said he hit me so hard that I flew across the room and burst my lip open.

This was a memory I had erased subconsciously and had obviously impacted me throughout my life. It probably had a lot to do with my anger issues and low self worth.

At least now I am aware and can contain those feelings.

For me I feel I have ridden the urge to drink again. If I can stay sober then my toxic anger cannot return.

I was always discontent with myself and others and hated the world.

Now is time for me to just be grateful for what I have and just settle down and be calm.

I hope someone can relate to my story and get something from it.

Printed in Great Britain
by Amazon